PATROL and TROOP LEADERSHIP

BOY SCOUTS OF AMERICA
North Brunswick, New Jersey

$1.25

CONTENTS

1972 Printing
Copyright 1972
Boy Scouts of America
North Brunswick, New Jersey
Library of Congress Catalog Card Number: 72-186627
ISBN 0-8395-6502-X
No. 6502   Printed U.S.A.   200M672

PART TWO—BEING A LEADER

PART ONE

LEADERSHIP

Chapter One

WHY LEADERSHIP?

ON most football teams the quarterback is the team leader. Why is that? Is there something magic about the position? Does he automatically become the leader—the guy who makes the team go—when he is named quarterback by the coach?

No, there's more to it than that. Lots more. Usually he is named quarterback because he's *already* a leader. He's al-

ready the kind of guy the other players like to follow.

And if the coach is wrong about him, he probably won't stay quarterback very long. If he can't lead the team, he won't have much value even if he can hit a receiver at 40 yards. Because every successful team *must* have a leader.

That goes for your Scouting team, too—your patrol and your troop. In fact, if the patrol and troop are to succeed, you need several leaders. Guys like yourself who want to try "quarterbacking" in Scouting. The aim of this book is to show you how to become a better leader.

Let's begin by being honest about it. This book is *not* going to make you a good leader. You are *not* going to find 5 or 10 simple rules to follow to become a good leader. If

leadership were as easy as that, almost everyone would be a good leader. And you know that most people are not.

There are no rules for leadership. But there are certain skills that every good leader seems to have. You will learn about them in this book and practice them in your patrol and troop.

Some of these skills you may already have—even without knowing it. That's the funny thing about leadership—a good leader doesn't necessarily know how he does it. He just does what comes naturally and the others follow him. Although he may not know it, he has mastered the skills of leadership.

As a patrol or troop leader you're going to learn what these skills are in a more scientific manner. You're going to learn what they are from this book and from troop leader training opportunities in your council or district.

Then you'll use these skills with your patrol and troop leaders' council.

This doesn't mean we guarantee that you'll be elected student council president next year. Or that you will be the Super Bowl quarterback 15 years from now or President of the United States in 35 years. But we do guarantee that you *can* make yourself a much better leader in just a few weeks or months.

What Is Leadership?

Leadership is a process of getting things done through people. The quarterback moves the team toward a touchdown. The senior patrol leader guides the troop to a high rating at the camporee. The mayor gets the people to support new policies to make the city better.

These leaders are getting things done by working through people—football players, Scouts, and ordinary citizens. They have used the process of leadership to reach certain goals.

Leadership is not a science. So being a leader is an adventure because you can never be sure whether you will reach your goal—at least this time. The touchdown drive may end in a fumble. The troop may have a bad weekend during the camporee. Or the city's citizens may not be convinced that the mayor's policies are right. So these leaders have to try again, using other methods. But they still use the same *process*—the process of good leadership.

Leadership means responsibility. It's adventure and often fun, but it always means responsibility. The leader is the guy the others look to to get the job done. So don't think your new job as a troop leader will be just an honor. It's more than that. It means that the other Scouts expect you to take the responsibility of getting the job done. If you lead, they will do the job. If you don't, they may expect you to do the job all by yourself.

That's why it's important that you begin right now to learn what leadership is all about.

Wear your badge of office proudly. It does not automatically make you a good leader. But it identifies you as a Scout who others *want* to follow—if you'll let them by showing leadership.

You are not a finished leader. No one ever is, not even a president or prime minister. But you are an explorer of the human mind because now you are going to try to learn how to get things done through people. This is one of the keys to leadership.

You are searching for the secrets of leadership. Many of them lie locked inside you. As you discover them and practice them, you will join a special group of people— skilled leaders.

Good exploring—both in this book and with the groups you will have a chance to lead.

THE
TASKS
OF
LEADERSHIP

Do you think that's true? Don't you believe it. It's true that chairmen, coaches, and kings lead, but people who hold no leadership position also lead. And you can find some people who have a leader's title and *ought* to lead. But they don't.

In other words, you're not a leader because you wear the leader's hat. Or because you wear the patrol leader's insignia on your uniform. You're a leader only when you are getting things done through other people.

Leadership, then, is something people do. Some people inherit leadership positions, such as kings, or nobles, or heads of family businesses. Some are elected: chairman, governor, patrol leader. Some are appointed, such as a coach, a city manager, or a den chief. Or they may just happen to be there when a situation arises that demands leadership. A disaster occurs, or a teacher doesn't show up when class begins, or a patrol leader becomes sick on a campout.

IN this section, we will consider several common statements about the people who serve in leadership positions throughout our world. After you have read the statement, decide for yourself whether you feel it is true or false and why you think it is.

Here's the first one. True or false?

The only people who lead have some kind of leadership job, such as chairman, coach, or king.

Try this statement. Is it true or false?

Leadership is a gift. If you're born with it, you can lead. If you're not, you can't.

Some people will tell you that. Some really believe it. But it's not so.

Leadership *does* take skill. Not everyone can learn all the skills of leadership as well as anyone else. But most people can learn some of them—and thus develop their own potential.

You don't have to be born with leadership. Chances are, you weren't. But you were born with a brain. If you can learn to swim or play checkers or do math, you can learn leadership skills.

True or false?

"Leader" is another word for "boss."

Well, what do you mean by "boss"? A guy who pushes and orders other people around? No, a leader is not one of those. (But some people try to lead this way.)

Or do you mean a boss is somebody who has a

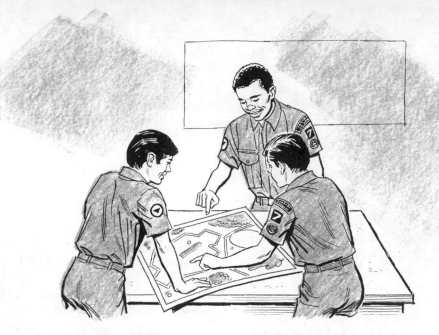

job to do and works with other people to get it done? This is true. A leader is a boss in that sense.

True or false?

Being a leader in a Scout troop is like being a leader anywhere else.

This one is true. When you lead in a Scout troop, you will do many of the same things as any leader anywhere.

The important thing now is Scouting gives you a chance to lead. You can learn *how* to lead in Scouting. You can *prac-*

tice leadership in Scouting. Then you can lead other groups, too. The skills you will need are very much the same.

What Does a Leader Deal With?

Every leader deals with just two things. Here they are. the *job* and the *group*.

The job is what's to be done. The "job" doesn't necessarily mean work. It could be playing a game. It could be building a skyscraper. It could be getting across an idea.

A leader is needed to get the job done. If there were no job, there would be no need for a leader.

The group, such as a patrol, is the people who do the job. And in many cases, the group continues after the job is done. This is where leading gets tough, as you'll see later.

Think about this situation. Mark has a lot of firewood to split. There he is, all alone with his ax. He's got a job to do. Is he a leader?

We have to say in this situation that Mark won't be leading. Why? No group. There's nobody on the job but Mark.

Here's another example: Danny and three of his friends are on their bikes. They have no place to go. They're just riding slowly, seeing how close they can get to each other.

Is Danny — or any one of the others — a leader?

From what we know, we have to say no. Why? No job. There's a group of friends, but nothing special to be done. You don't need a leader for that.

(You don't need a group, either.)

The Job of a Leader

A leader works with two things: a job and a group. You can always tell when a leader succeeds, because:

1. The job gets done.

2. The group holds together.

Let's see why it takes both.

Frank was elected patrol leader. That same week, the patrol had a job cleaning up an old cemetery.

It was Frank's first leadership position, and he wanted it to go right. In his daydream he could see the Scoutmaster praising him for the great cleanup job. So when Saturday morning came, Frank and the patrol went over to the cemetery, and Frank started to get the job done.

He hollered. He yelled. He threatened. He called them names. He worked like a tiger himself. It was a rough day, but the cemetery got cleaned up.

Frank went home sort of proud, sort of mad, and very tired.

"How'd things go, Frank?" the Scoutmaster asked a few days later.

"Good."

"No problems?"

"No." Frank wondered what he meant by that.

"Oh! Well, a couple of the boys in your patrol asked me if they could change to another patrol. I thought maybe something had gone wrong...."

And that was how Frank learned that getting the job done isn't all

that's not leadership. The group must go on.

Another new patrol leader called a meeting at his house. Everybody seemed to be hungry when they came. So they got some snacks from the kitchen. Then they tossed a football around. It began to get dark, and one by one they went home. Everybody had fun. But the patrol meeting — the job — never started.

One of the following statements is the message of this part of the book. Which one?

a. Nice guys finish last.
b. Mean guys finish last.
c. Leaders get the job done and keep the group going.
d. Leaders have a special title or badge that makes others like to follow.

We'll take the third one. Will you?

What Affects Leadership?

Leadership is not magic that comes out of a leader's head. It's skill. The leader learns how to get the job done and still keep the group together.

there is to leadership. He had really given the group a hard time, and now they wanted to break up.

Almost anybody with a whip and a mean temper can get a job done. But in doing it, they usually destroy the group. And

Does this mean that the leader does the same things in every situation? No. Here's why.

Leadership differs with the *leader*, the *group*, and the *situation*.

Leaders — like other people — are all different. No leader can take over another leader's job and do it the same way.

Groups are different, too. A great football coach might have difficulty leading an orchestra. A good sergeant might be a poor Scoutmaster. So when a leader changes groups, he changes the way he leads.

Situations differ, too. The same leader with the same group must change with conditions. A fellow leading a group discussion needs to change his style of leadership when a fire breaks out. As a Scout leader, you probably can't lead the group in the rain the same as you do in the sunshine.

An effective leader, then, must be alert at all times to the reaction of the members of the group; the conditions in which he may find himself; and be aware of his own abilities and reactions.

Leadership Develops

Picture a long scale like a yardstick. On the low end, there are no leadership skills. On the other end, there is a complete set of leadership skills.

Everyone is somewhere between those ends!

Where do you find yourself at this time? Unknowingly, you may be further up the scale than you realize. As a patrol or troop leader you'll now have the opportunity to find out.

How Will You Know You're Improving?

You learn leadership best by working with groups. That is something like learning swimming best by getting into the water.

Yet you can't keep track of your progress without a guide. You must know and understand what you're trying to learn. This means you have to know what the skills of leadership are.

Chapter Three

THE SKILLS OF

LEADERSHIP

LEADING makes use of many skills. We are going to take up nine of them here. These nine skills are presented in leadership courses you may take as a patrol or troop leader.

These nine skills are most important. Many of them intertwine. Some cannot be used alone. If you can improve your skill in each of the nine, you'll improve your effectiveness as a leader.

With each skill, we'll follow this pattern:

- An example of the skill in use
- An explanation of the skill
- A use of the skill

- How to evaluate whether you're improving in that skill

Communications [Getting and Giving Information]

A patrol leader sent two Scouts on an errand from camp. Rusty and Bruce did fine until they came to a stream.

"Hey, where ya goin'?"

"He said turn left."

"He did not. He said turn right here."

"No, that was back there. By the clearing. He said when we get to the stream, we turn left."

"No he didn't. But go ahead, wise guy. I'll see you there."

So Rusty turned right and Bruce turned left. They were soon out of sight of each other. Bruce followed directions and reached their destination in a few minutes. When he arrived there, he found no Rusty. Half an hour later, still no Rusty. Bruce finally raced down the trail back to camp, got help, and they began searching. It took 2 hours to find Rusty. He had taken the wrong turn at the stream, soon lost the trail, and couldn't get back.

Why did this happen? Here are some possibilities. Which do you think was the problem:

- Rusty didn't listen to the patrol leader's instructions.
- Rusty thought he understood the directions when he really didn't.
- The patrol leader gave poor directions.
- The patrol leader should have made sure both boys knew the directions.

Now let's consider each of these statements.

Rusty didn't listen. This may be true. But the patrol leader didn't know that Rusty didn't listen or, at least, he didn't find out whether he did or not.

Rusty thought he understood. This is probably

true. He was pretty convinced when he argued with Bruce. But we must ask how the patrol leader managed to let him go away with the wrong idea.

The patrol leader gave poor directions. Bruce got them right, so they were OK to him. But since only one of the two boys understood the directions, we have to suspect that they might not have been perfectly clear.

The patrol leader should have made sure. This is certainly true. If he had made Rusty repeat the directions, he would have found where "right" replaced "left."

Whatever happened, we need look at the results.

Information wasn't given and received properly. The job didn't get done. (And the search for Rusty prevented some other jobs from getting done.) Besides, the confused information began to affect the way members of the group felt about each other. This kind of thing threatens the group morale and effectiveness.

How could this misunderstanding—of one word—have been prevented? Check any of the following that would have helped if the patrol leader had done them:

- He made sure both boys were paying attention before he gave directions.
- He spoke slowly and clearly.
- He had Rusty and Bruce make a diagram and write the directions in a notebook.
- He had the boys repeat their instructions.

You probably checked all of them. And you're right. Any *one* of them might have prevented the misunderstanding.

Notice that leaders both give and get information. Communication happens both ways.

How can you apply these ideas in your leadership tasks? Easy. To improve your skills in *getting* information, follow these rules:

- Pay attention and listen carefully.
- Make notes and sketches.

- Ask questions and repeat your understanding of what was said.

To improve your skills in *giving* information, there is a similar set of guidelines:

- Make sure the others are listening before you start giving information.
- Speak slowly and clearly.
- Draw diagrams and pictures and have those receiving the instructions make notes.
- Have the others repeat back their understanding of the information.

From time to time you can check yourself to see whether you are improving in the skill of getting and giving information. Ask yourself these questions:

- Are your Scouts forgetting less?
- Do they take notes regularly?
- Do they ask questions when in doubt?
- Do you take notes yourself and review them to be sure you don't forget things?

Knowing [and Using] the Resources of the Group

Most of the members of the Owl Patrol were new Scouts. Harry, the patrol leader, thought the Scouts should be trained to pitch tents just before their first campout. He picked Phil to run the demonstration because he was aggressive and always seemed sure of himself.

Much to Harry's surprise, Phil's tent-pitching demonstration was a bust. It was pretty clear to all that Phil didn't know which part of the tent to fasten down and which part to put up in the air. But Bob, another patrol member, helped Phil out and soon had it going right. Then Bob helped the others set up their tents.

Later on, Harry learned that Bob had done a lot of weekend camping with his family and knew a lot about tents. But why had he picked Phil to do the demonstration?

Harry probably thought that Phil, being as confi-

dent as he was, could handle it. It never occurred to him that Phil didn't know anything about tents. And because Bob was quieter, it didn't enter Harry's mind that he had some skills.

Harry didn't learn about Bob's knowledge and skill as a camper until it was almost too late. How could he have avoided embarrassing Phil in front of the patrol?

As patrol leader, Harry needed to know what resources were available to him. A resource is a thing you can use. A book, a tool, a piece of wood, or a handful of sand may be a resource. People can also be resources, because:

• They know how to do things.

• They have information or knowledge.

• They know how and where to get other resources.

Every member of every group is some kind of resource. Not everyone has something to give to every job, but each member of a group should be encouraged to add what he can.

From our example, it is clear that Harry needed to learn the resources of each of the members of his patrol. How might he have done this? Here are four ways:

- Through observation. In the case of Phil, Harry had seen him as a resource because he was always self-confident. But he was the wrong resource for that job. Later, Harry learned that Bob knew a lot about putting up tents. But the big disadvantage of this method is that it takes so long. You may make a lot of mistakes before you find out what resources everyone has.

- You may find out various Scouts' interests and skills by casual talk with them. Or you may hear about it from some other person. But this is also a slow way to find out what you need to know.

- You can ask questions. Harry might have asked his patrol who had experience in tent pitching. He probably would have discovered Bob's skill in this way.

• Give each member of the group a resource sheet with specific questions on it. For instance, it could read, "Check below all of the skills you think you are pretty good at: knot tying, nature lore, hiking, cooking, etc." The resource sheet might also include a suggestion that members of the group show which skills they think they could help others to learn.

However you find the resources in your group, make notes of them in your notebook or keep a card file of personal resources. Don't trust your memory.

How much do you know about the Scouts in your patrol or troop? What would it be helpful to know? Their special skills? Their past experiences? Their hopes and fears? Their weaknesses as well as their strengths? Goals? Attitudes? Find out these things and keep a record.

It may be that you will sometimes find ways to strengthen other Scouts by helping them learn to do things they have had little chance to do. You

may give them experiences doing things they may have been afraid to do. In such ways your resource knowledge works to benefit each Scout.

From time to time, check over your resource file and ask yourself whether you're keeping it updated. Has your patrol program improved through your use of the information recorded on each boy's card? Are you helping him to grow? Has knowing these resources made you a better leader?

A leader must know the resources of his group. He can never know too many. Every time there is a job, some of these resources should be used. Which ones? The ones that will (1) get the job done and (2) keep the group together.

Setting the Example

A den chief came to a den meeting without his uniform. A week later, two of the Cub Scouts appeared out of uniform.

"Why?" demanded the Den Mother.

"Bill didn't wear his last week."

Bill never said to any of the Cub Scouts, "It's

OK if you don't wear your uniform sometimes." But that was the message that came through. His good example of coming in uniform broke down only once. That was enough for a couple of his group.

Which is stronger, good or bad example? We can't always be sure. Setting a good example will often not work all by itself. But if you exchange it for a bad example, you may get immediate action (of the wrong kind).

Alan was elected senior patrol leader. He took his new job very seriously. If there was ever any horseplay, he stayed out of it. He felt he had to in order not to set a bad example.

On one camping trip the patrol leaders got some horseplay going after "Taps," and Alan joined in. Everybody had a ball.

The next day, every one of the patrols got completely out of hand. The Scoutmaster finally had to step in and settle everyone down. Then he and Alan had a talk.

"That's the first time I've done anything like that since I was elected," Alan complained.

"What effect do you think it had?" asked the Scoutmaster.

"I don't know. There's been a little trouble before, but never like this. They always knew I wouldn't put up with it."

"Always until when?"

"Until... well, until last night. I guess I showed 'em a little fooling around is OK."

Thus, Alan learned to keep a good example going. Even if it seemed not to do much good. Because a bad example would almost certainly make things worse.

People learn from models and examples. I show you my square knot. I untie it and tie it slowly while you watch. Then you try to tie a knot like mine.

We use models in teaching because they work. Models let people know what we want. Models say, "Here, do it like this."

People are models themselves. A girl models a dress for a customer.

The message is, "If you'll buy this dress, you'll be as beautiful as me."

A leader is a model whether he wants to be or not. He doesn't have to tell the group to follow his example. In fact, he can even tell them not to follow his example, but they will.

"What you are speaks so loudly I cannot hear what you say," said Emerson.

Setting an example is more than staying out of trouble. It is an important element in leadership. It is showing the way. It is an active process that raises standards and goals. It is a great deal more than just avoiding the wrong things. Setting an example means doing the right things, and knowing why.

As a leader, you are observed by others at all times. Other Scouts are watching you and learning to do what you do. Are you proud of what they see? How can you set a good example?

Follow instructions. There's at least one right way to do everything. There may be a dozen wrong ways to do each. Don't expect others to do things right if you don't.

Try harder. If you'll settle for last place, so will the group. Get up earlier and run faster than anybody. They can't follow you if you're not out ahead.

Take the initiative. Shakespeare wrote, "Some are born great, some achieve greatness, and some have greatness thrust upon them." Don't wait for leadership to be thrust upon you. Find out what has to happen and make it happen.

Act mature. If you act like a half-wit, you'll be a good model for those trying to win the half-wit badge. That's not what your group needs. You'll get a lot more respect by acting mature than by being a silly kid.

Know your job. Never quit trying to do a better job. Know your group and its resources. Pick up new skills and improve on old ones. You can't learn too much about leadership. (But it's very easy to learn too little.)

Make a special effort to conduct yourself at home, school, and during Scout activities so that you will be pleased when others follow your example. How you act includes what you say and do and how you dress. It includes your attitudes and how you relate to others.

As you work at improving your example as a leader, you should take stock from time to time. What new area can you develop? How is your conduct in meetings of the troop and the troop leaders' council? What kinds of attitudes are others "catching" from you?

Representing the Group

At the troop leaders' council meeting, Charlie, the Fox Patrol leader, voted for the hike to Donner's Mill with great enthusiasm. He thought it would be a great hike. At a later troop meeting, the senior patrol leader announced the hike to Donner's Mill and there was a loud groan from the Foxes. The Scoutmaster and senior patrol leader were quite surprised, since Charlie had been so enthusiastic.

What made the Foxes react in that way? Did they have a better location in mind? Had they

grown tired of Donner's Mill for some reason? Most likely, they just wished they had been consulted. Charlie just hadn't represented them. He had spoken for himself, not his patrol.

In a pure democracy, everyone speaks for himself. No one is ever appointed to speak for anyone else. Thus, everyone has to be consulted before anything is done.

There aren't many pure democracies, because it is almost impossible to get very much done. The bigger the group, the less possible it becomes to have a pure democracy.

To overcome these problems, we have representative democracies. A Scout troop is an example of one. The patrol leaders are the representatives of the patrol. They speak for the members of their patrol.

Suppose you are a patrol member. The patrol is going to elect a leader. Three members of your patrol are candidates. You don't know which one to vote for.

Each candidate is asked to state what he understands about representing his patrol at the troop leaders' council. Which of the following boys would get your vote?

SAM: Look, man, if you elect me, you gotta trust me to do what's right. I know what you guys want. I won't let you down.

PAT: I don't agree with Sam. I don't think he knows what you want. I don't know either. But any time there's a question, we'll take a vote. Majority rules. I'll speak for the side with the most votes. Isn't that fair?

TIM: No, it's not fair. I think the leader should speak for everybody, not just the majority. If five of you vote for A and only two of you vote for B, I think the two should be heard too. If you elect me, I'll speak for everybody, whether we all agree or not.

You can vote the way you please, but...

1. Sam will speak for himself. When his views and yours are the same, he'll be representing you. When they're different, your views won't be represented.

2. Pat will represent your views whenever they're on the majority side. If less than half of the patrol thinks your way, you won't be represented.

3. Tim will represent you every time — even

when he doesn't agree with you.

You Can Count on This. — You can't represent a group unless you know what they think. And you can't know what they think unless you ask them.

Here are some suggestions for asking:

Get the facts. Do you understand what they're telling you? Do they understand what they're being asked about?

Analyze the situation. If there's a problem, can it be handled inside the group? Or must other leaders be brought in?

Get the group's reaction. If all feel the same way, fine. If there's a difference of opinion, find out all sides of it.

Take notes. You can't remember all details long enough to represent the group. Write them down. Read them back to the group to be sure you haven't left out anything.

When You Represent the Group. — Make sure you get all the information, opinions, and ideas of your group before speaking for it.

Give the facts. If there are different points of view, state them. Give the reason for them. Present them so fairly that no one will know which side you favor.

Respect their opinions. Your group may all agree on something. Other groups may agree on the opposite. Listen to what they have to say. They may have information your group did not know about.

Represent some things in private. When there's some personality problem in your group, present it to one or two leaders. Don't hang it out for everyone to see.

Take notes. You will have to report back to your group. They will want to know what happened and why. Write it down so you won't forget anything.

Have you been elected patrol leader? How can you best represent your patrol at the troop leaders' council and the council to your patrol? Some possibilities are (1) give the facts, (2) respect others' opinions, (3) represent some things in private, and (4) take notes.

As you practice the skills noted above, you need to evaluate your progress. Are you giving every patrol member a chance to express his opinion? Do you report opinions different from your own? Do you present the opinions of others fairly or slant them to your own opinions?

Evaluation

Do you recall the last time a skill was demonstrated at a troop meeting? How did it go? Who did it? Do you think you could do as well? Better? Quite a bit better? There you go — evaluating. And it's all based on your personal values.

"Boy, I wish I was as good a patrol leader as Pete."

"Look at those Foxes. The Owls can do a lot better than that."

"We made a few mistakes this time, but watch out for us at the next camporee!"

The easiest evaluation for a leader is to trust his own judgment. That's also the worst. What the leader thinks and what the group thinks are often far apart.

Years ago a survey was made of Scout camps. Camp leaders were asked how they thought the Scouts liked various camp activities. The Scouts were asked how they liked the same ones.

The results showed that the camp leaders weren't very good at guessing what the Scouts liked. For example, leaders rated religious services in camp as very low in popularity. Scouts rated them very high. Camp leaders rated big, mass activities as most popular among Scouts. But the Scouts said the things they liked best were the ones they did in small groups.

Everything your patrols and troop do should be evaluated. But not by you alone; let the Scouts who take part in them share their thoughts with you.

But you have to be sure you understand what they're telling you.

Here are some pointers that will help you understand the answers you get from the Scouts.

1. *People's personal values show.* Each person sees things in his own way. The boy who loves water sports may not think much of camping on the desert. That doesn't mean he's wrong. It just helps you to understand how he evaluates 3 days on very dry land.

2. *When you ask for facts you need simple answers.* This means that you will have to ask questions that will get simple answers.

This type of question will get a simple answer: How many patrol meetings should there be every month?

On the other hand, this question will *not* get a simple answer: Why do you think your patrol should meet once a week?

3. *A person seldom tells how he really feels with short answers.* If you want to know how many or how much, short answers are fine. If you want to know how people really feel, you have to give them freedom to answer.

Which of the following questions leaves the person the greatest freedom to tell how he feels?

a. Did you enjoy the last camp-out?

b. Would you rather fish or play golf?

c. How do you think we could improve our camping program?

(The first two questions above allow only one possible answer each, and they don't tell us why. You can say anything you want to answer the third.)

4. *Some situations prevent honest answers.* When a person feels threatened, he will not evaluate honestly. The newest Scout in your troop probably will not answer questions frankly until he feels that he belongs. A newly appointed quartermaster is not going to evaluate the senior patrol leader's (SPL) recommendation too critically until they have worked together for a time and he has become better acquainted with the job.

You may want to try some group evaluation in your patrol the next time you have an activity. Were all members present? If not, why? What did the patrol get done? Did they enjoy doing it? Will they do it again? How could the activity have been improved?

To check your ability in this skill, you must decide just how you are using evaluation to help you lead better. Do you listen to what is said? Do you make excuses for doing what you do?

Summary:

• *You can't stay on the*

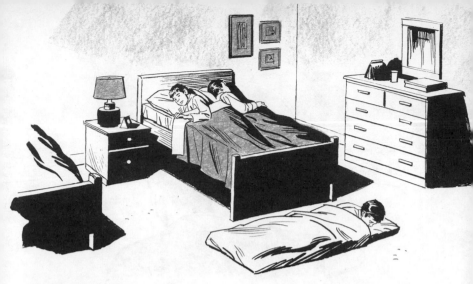

track unless you know where you are going and then evaluate what you are doing successfully to get there.

- *Find out from others how you're doing. Don't just trust your own judgment.*
- *Be sure you know what you're asking.*
- *Be sure you know what they're telling you.*

Planning

A Scout troop recently made a bus tour of the Southeast. Most nights the troop camped in parks and campgrounds. The four patrols set up their camps in their usual fashion without difficulty.

One night the troop stayed in a motel. The Scoutmaster told the senior patrol leader that five boys would sleep in each of seven rooms. He then gave the SPL the task of assigning boys to rooms.

The SPL laid out seven pieces of paper and announced that Scouts should sign up for their rooms and select their own room leader.

Before the Scouts began moving into the rooms the Scoutmaster asked to see the room assignments. The SPL was very proud of what he had done and handed over the signup sheets. The Scoutmaster then dis-

covered that two rooms had only five boys between them, and five boys had no place to sleep at all. Of course, the problem was quickly solved, but how did it come about in the first place? Poor planning!

Someone must have known in advance that staying in the motel would involve different arrangements than the usual patrol setup. You can't just pull into a motel and register 40 people in an instant. How could it have been handled better?

In this case the troop leaders' council should have done the planning, not just one person. The first task was to consider the situation: 35 boys in seven rooms, each room with a room leader. Next, the resources should have been reviewed: five beds in a room, four patrols of eight boys plus the SPL, assistant SPL, and quartermaster. (Do you see an obvious plan already?)

Planning is almost always faster and easier if you know what you're planning. More specifically, you have to know what you're trying to accomplish. So in considering the task, think about the outcomes. What do you want to happen? What will be the result? Will there be more than one desired result? If so, will they conflict?

As a plan develops, you need to consider al-

ternates. (For instance, what would this troop have done if it turned out that some rooms held four and others six?) Have a Plan B ready in case something upsets your plan.

Finish your plan, make assignments, and write the plan down so everyone can understand it.

To plan anything, follow this course:

- Consider the task.
- Consider the resources.
- Consider alternatives.
- Reach a decision.
- Write it down and review it with the group.
- Carry out the plan.

You can use these steps in planning just about anything: a hike,

teaching a skill at a troop meeting, a window display, summer camp, a service project. After a while the six steps will come to you naturally.

Improve every time you plan by evaluating what you did last time. How can you do it better? Did you use all available resources? How do you know? Were all alternatives considered? Did everyone participate? Did they enjoy it? Were they satisfied with the outcome? Did everyone understand the plan?

Control

George is a senior patrol leader. At a camporee, the troop was packing its gear, getting ready to leave. The equipment was spread out on the ground, and each of the five patrols was assembled around its equipment.

The senior patrol leader was barking out instructions: "Trail Chef Kit — first, the large pot." In turn, each patrol leader would shout to his patrol to come up with the large pot.

Seeing each patrol leader with the large pot in hand, George would bellow out the next order:

"Four aluminum plates in the bottom!" Then each patrol leader would respond, the plates would be found and inserted, and the next command would follow. So it went through the folding of the tents and the storing of all equipment. The task was finally completed, and everything was in its proper place. But long before the job was finished many of the Scouts were horsing around, learning nothing about camp housekeeping or, for that matter, responsibility.

In managing the job this way, George had the task under control but not the troop. He had lost sight of the people while he got the job done. How might he have done it?

At the troop leaders' council meeting he should have reminded the patrol leaders of the task of putting away equipment properly. When the time came to do it, he should have been casually observing the patrols as they went about it. Where it was being done quickly and well, he would comment on the good job being done and go on. If he found problems, he would offer to help, give the patrol leader a hand, or perhaps note how it might be done better. If he encountered disagreements about how to do it, he would resolve them.

So we see that control is not being a dictator. Rather, it is using good sense and skill to get the job done and keep the group together. Briefly stated, control consists of:

- Observing the group.
- Making instructions fit the situation.

- Helping where necessary.
- Examining the completed work.
- Reacting to the quality of the work.

Your next patrol or troop activity will give you a chance to try this system. How will you know how successful you were? Ask yourself these questions afterward. Did the job get done on time? How do you feel about it? How do your group members feel? Did you help those who needed it? How did others react? Will the group do better because of this experience? Why?

Successful control gets the job done at the right time, at the right place, and in the right way. But more, it encourages the group to do better next time.

Sharing Leadership

Last week the patrol of which Jim is the leader made plans for their part in the troop's 3-day canoe trip. All nine members were present and all had a part in developing the plans. The overall plan had already been made by the troop leaders' council, so the patrol had to stay within that plan in making their own. By the time the patrol meeting broke up, every member had taken on some responsibility for the trip, either before it or during it.

A day or so before they left, Jim called each member to check on his progress. Everyone was all set except Bill. He was to act as tour navigator, but he hadn't got the maps he needed. With Jim's questioning, he admitted he hadn't done much about trying to get them.

Jim then wanted to know how he planned to carry out his navigator duties if he had no maps. "Oh, I thought we'd just follow another patrol," Bill replied.

"How do you think our guys will like that?"

"Not so great I guess. What do you think I should do?" Bill sounded a little bit defeated.

"We still have a day and a half before the trip, why don't you call the

Scoutmaster and see if he has any maps. If he doesn't, you can try Mr. Jones, who's on the troop committee. I'm sure they'll get the maps for you. Next time you have a job to do, let me know if you need help."

"OK, Jim, I'll get 'em. Don't worry."

Although Jim is the elected patrol leader, he chose to share his leadership in several ways in this situation. Did you notice how?

At the beginning, he allowed every member to take part in planning. He had to set the limits, be- cause some things had already been decided, but within those limits, he let them plan.

Second, he had everyone share in the responsibility for a successful trip. Everyone had a job to do and, thereby, felt a part of the team.

As leader, Jim was smart enough to check on everyone. When he found Bill hadn't done his job, he had two alternatives. He could have taken over and got the maps. Or he could persuade Bill to do his job. That was the course he chose. Do you think it was the right one?

There are two other ways in which Jim might have shared leadership. One would be the "iron hand" type where he would simply tell the patrol what was expected of them. This is the least desirable for the growth of the members and the group, but it is sometimes necessary with a weak or inexperienced group or in the event of an emergency.

Another approach is for the leader to join the group as an equal and not play any leadership role at all. This is a good style for discussion but

is not the right approach for most situations.

As a leader, you can share tasks but never share responsibility. If you assign John to cut the firewood, the task is his but the responsibility is yours. If John doesn't have a pile of wood ready when it's needed, you will not get off the hook by saying, "Well I gave that job to John, and it's his fault that there's no wood." If there is no wood, it's your fault. Giving the job to someone doesn't end your responsibility. It ends only when the job is done satisfactorily.

43

Good leadership — using several styles and approaches — will produce such results as these:

- A spirit of cooperation
- Teamwork
- A feeling on the part of each member that he is needed and wanted.

With good leadership, members of the group will continue to grow in their development as individuals because they are made to feel that they are accountable for their actions.

In your next few opportunities to lead, try using some or all of the various styles of leadership. They refer to the extent of sharing of leadership with the group, and are listed in order from the least to the most sharing:

- Telling
- Persuading
- Consulting
- Delegating
- Joining

When you have given several of these a try, then ask yourself these questions. Do you use more than one comfortably? How do you really feel about sharing leader-

Name	Duties
Joe	tentage
Mike	food, rolls, meat
John	Water can
Dick	blankets, axes
Jim	Maps, compass
Harry	Camping permits

ship with the group? Do you get better results with one or more methods? How does the patrol react to each style of leadership you use? Can you combine methods?

Managing Learning

For a patrol hike, Mike had been made responsible for bringing the hamburger buns. He got them in plenty of time and put them in the freezer to keep them fresh for Saturday. When the patrol reached its destination on the big day, everybody began pulling out their part of the patrol's lunch. It wasn't until Mike reached for the hamburger buns that he remembered that they were still home in the freezer! And there was just no way to get back or to get some substitutes.

At the time it wasn't a laughing matter, but by the next meeting of the troop, Mike and his patrol leader Tom were having a good laugh as they told the story to Carl, the senior patrol leader.

"What'd you learn from that?" Carl asked them.

"Not to forget the hamburger buns!" was Mike's instant reply.

"Sure," laughed Carl, "but is that all?" He seemed to be looking straight at Tom.

"Well, I guess it was my fault — I didn't check up on Mike. He agreed to bring the buns, and I let it go at that."

Carl pressed a little further. "How will you handle things like this another time?"

"Well, I guess I'd better keep a list of responsibilities and review them with those on the list before we get going," said Tom.

"OK, that's good," responded Carl. "Now how about you, Mike? What did you learn?"

"Well, I made a list of what I was to bring. But Saturday morning I didn't read it over carefully. And I should have checked off the items when I had them packed."

Thus, a simple matter of forgotten buns was made into a real learning experience. Let's review just what Carl did to bring this about.

First, he noticed that the two boys (and the whole patrol, for that matter) had had what can be called "a guided discovery." They had been in the middle of something and they knew about it firsthand.

Second, he had Tom and Mike review the experience and helped them to realize that they had learned something that could be applied to other situations. They hadn't learned that hamburgers need rolls but about how to get things done.

Third, he had them think about how they would apply what they had learned next time.

The final step would be to evaluate the learning. That could only happen next time. If Mike was more careful about reading his checklist or if Tom was more thorough about checking up on his patrol members, they would know that learning had really occurred.

We call this process "managing learning." In this case it was Carl who did the managing. He took advantage of a situation that had already happened. If he had ignored it or just had a good laugh about Mike's forgetfulness, there might have been little or no learning.

You can use this same method to help almost anybody learn almost anything. We'll take another example and see how you can use the method.

Suppose a camporee is coming up. There is to be a competitive event involving use of the map and compass. You think your patrol members are a little rusty on that. Here's how you might proceed.

STEP ONE: *Guided Discovery*

Provide each member of the patrol with a compass and have each one orient a map and plot a course that you specify. Watch how they do. Some may do well. Others will get off to a bad start and fumble. Out of this, you will know just who needs to learn what. But equally important is that the learner "discovers" his shortcomings or unforgotten skills.

STEP TWO: *Teaching-Learning*

You or someone you share leadership with gives instructions and information about the map and compass task. Let them practice each step as you describe or demonstrate it. When you feel certain the learners know the skills, you allow them to progress to the next phase. Some learners may reach this step faster than others—that's

just fine—let them progress at their own speed.

STEP THREE: *Application*

Have the learners do a series of problems with map and compass. If they are successful, they go on. If not, you take them back through some of the teaching-learning process until they can be successful.

STEP FOUR: *Evaluation*

This process occurs every step of the way, but it's important to review all four steps when you are through. As learners are called on to perform, you must decide whether they are performing acceptably. Have each learner express himself about what he thinks he has learned. Ask questions, such as:

"Do you feel you know this skill well enough to do it again next week?"

"Could you help one of the others here who is having trouble learning the skill?"

"Could you teach someone else to do it?"

PART TWO

BEING A LEADER

Chapter Four

LEADERSHIP

IN THE PATROL

ON the first day of the world's first Scout troop, the members organized patrols. Robert Baden-Powell, the founder of Scouting, wanted to try out the program "officially" for the first time. So he and 20 boys, who didn't even know each other, headed for Brownsea Island for a week of camping and Scouting.

Baden-Powell had developed a type of Scouting years earlier as a military training method for men. After he wrote a book about it, his Scouting was taken up by boys as a game—most of them with no adult leaders. At Brownsea Island, Baden-Powell tried out what the boys had been doing on their own.

The patrol was a natural part of the program. Without it, the troop would be just another gang of boys organized and led by men. Baden-Powell knew that boys could lead themselves. But for this to happen, they had to be organized into a group of a size that boys were used to.

A patrol offers four special things to its members:

- Every boy has a say in the doings of the patrol.
- Boys learn to work together and do things well.
- They get a chance to learn and practice the skills of leadership and membership.
- They learn to take care of each other.

The last two chapters explain this about a patrol: It has jobs to do, and it's a group to be kept together. The jobs come in the form of activities, projects, and meetings. If the members of the patrol do these jobs with a positive attitude, they will find themselves enjoying each other and the task...it's fun! The fun keeps the group together — nobody would want to leave and miss any of the fun.

We'll think about the patrol leader's job later in this chapter. Right now, let's consider the group that we call a patrol.

The Membership of the Patrol

A patrol can be any size from about 5 to 10 Scouts. Patrols usually have to have at least five to be big enough to do much. As they get bigger than 10, patrols often get too big to handle.

Any boy qualified to be a Scout can belong to a patrol. Members are usually age 11 to 14.

A patrol works best if its members enjoy being together, so they should have something in common. What they usually have in common is that they know each other outside the patrol. They may live in the same neighborhood. They may go to the same school. They may go fishing or play ball together.

It's possible to make a patrol out of a group of strangers. But it's a lot harder. You might as well take advantage of any friendships or common interests they have.

Allow Scouts in a troop to form their own groups. They will always do it by friendship. So why do it on any other basis?

The New Boy.—How does a boy join the troop? Easy. He joins a patrol. The best way is for members to invite friends to join the patrol. Most boys are happy to be asked...and many are just waiting for the invitation.

But what about the new boy who just shows up at the troop meeting? Nobody has invited him to join. What patrol does he join? The troop leaders' council should decide on the basis of:

- Any preference the boy himself may have.
- Which patrols have members who know him.
- Which patrols have room for more.

Once in a while a new boy will appear at a troop meeting who is unknown to anyone. In that case, it makes sense to have him invited by a patrol that has members who live near him.

Even more rarely, a boy will appear who is not popular with anyone. This is where the patrol leader reminds everyone what Scout spirit means. Some patrol has the job of making the boy feel welcome. They may not like it, but they do it. "A Scout is friendly."

Patrol Organization.—The patrol has only one long-term leader: the patrol leader. He is elected from the membership of the patrol by the patrol itself. The recommended term of office is 6 months.

Patrol leaders must meet the qualifications set by the troop leaders' council. For example, if the troop leaders' council should decide that patrol leaders must be at least 12 years old and at least First Class, then no one could be elected unless he qualified in those ways. Your own troop leaders' council decides these things.

The patrol leader chooses his own assistant patrol leader for any length of time (within his own term of office). He also assigns other jobs in the patrol as needed. He may appoint a quartermaster or a scribe for a single event or over a period of time. He may appoint a song leader for an evening. He gets the job done, using the resources of the patrol.

The main reason for being so flexible is to allow the patrol leader to use the resources of his patrol well. He can meet changing situations. He can give each member of the patrol a chance to take on certain jobs, to give him the experience. For example, every member of your patrol could, at one time or another, serve as assistant patrol leader.

Patrol Meetings and Activities

Your patrol succeeds when it does interesting things as a patrol. It fails as a patrol when it does nothing interesting or, worse yet, when it does nothing. If you meet for a few minutes within regular troop meetings but do nothing else as a patrol, you won't get far.

However, a new patrol can't just start out doing things on its own. Some other things have to happen first.

- Your patrol will have to discover that it needs to do things outside troop meetings and that it needs help in getting started.

- Your patrol will then have to get the help it needs — to plan an activity, to learn some skills, or whatever is needed. Your senior patrol leader, members of the leadership corps, adult leaders, or others are qualified and ready to help.

- Your patrol will have to show by its

actions that it is ready and willing to work as a patrol team and that you can be counted on to do a job as a patrol.

A young, inexperienced patrol belongs close to home and close to the troop. As it matures, it can do more activities on its own, away from home. It becomes able to meet separately, on its own. As leaders and parents gain confidence in your patrol's ability, you may be allowed the privilege of hiking and even camping on your own.

But keep in mind—

- Your patrol must prove to *itself* that it can succeed on its own.
- Your patrol must prove to *adult leaders* and *parents* that it can succeed on its own.

Let's see how a patrol grows up through meetings and activities.

Troop Meetings.—Most troops have more meetings than any other kind of activity. This is where the members of the patrol can begin to learn what they can do as a patrol.

Here are some things a patrol can do — as a patrol — at troop meetings. There are many, many more.

- Set up the meeting place and put it in order afterward.
- Run games and ceremonies.
- Put on skill demonstrations.
- Compete against other patrols.
- Make plans for other activities.
- Work on advancement.

Can you think of some others?

If you have responsibility for planning troop meetings, be sure they're planned to keep the patrols active. Troop meetings without patrol activities may soon destroy the patrols. Almost every activity in a troop meeting can strengthen the patrols. For instance:

- Uniform inspection can be competitive among patrols.
- Contests and games can be competitive among patrols.
- Planning for other troop activities should be done by the patrols and with the patrols in mind.
- Patrols can be given responsibility for major parts of each troop meeting.

The Troop's Outdoor Program.—The troop's outdoor program should help to develop stronger patrols. Let's take two examples and see how they affect patrols.

EXAMPLE ONE: *A Weekend Camp-Out*

Planning. The patrols are represented on the troop leaders' council by their patrol leaders. They plan the what, when, and where for the troop.

The patrols themselves plan their part in the camp-out: menu, food buying activities, equipment, and perhaps transportation.

You will find lots of good suggestions to guide your patrol to prepare for hiking and camping in such books as the *Fieldbook* and the *Camping*, *Hiking*, and *Cooking* merit badge pamphlets, in addition to the *Scout Handbook.*

In camp, patrols prepare their own campsite, fireplace, and latrine. They set up their tents and other gear. The patrol leader assigns members to gather wood, prepare the meals, and clean up afterward.

In the total program, patrols play many important parts. They may put on demonstrations, compete with other patrols, organize patrol hikes, work on advancement together, make up games, or put on patrol campfires.

EXAMPLE TWO: *Summer Camp*

The same kinds of patrol activity should come about before and during summer camp — but lots more of them. There's more planning to be done. Instead of 1 or 2 days of activity, there are 6 or more.

The patrol really comes into its own in summer camp. Even a young, inexperienced patrol can grow up in summer camp.

You shouldn't think that just going camping will really make your patrol into something great. It depends on how and where you do your camping. Here are some tips on camping that will increase your fun and strengthen your patrol.

Do it yourselves. Ask for real responsibility for the patrols — don't expect the adult Scout leaders to do it for you. Get your patrol going and show the men what you can do by yourselves. They'll believe it when they see it...and be mighty proud of you!

Get under canvas. Resist the temptation to sleep in cabins and call it camping. Get outdoors where your patrol has to really do things to make itself comfortable. You don't exactly put your best skills to the test when you toss your sleeping bag on a ready-made bunk in a heated cabin!

Cook your own chow. It may be easier to have the adult leaders do the cooking, but you'll never make a real patrol out of your gang unless they learn to work together and put on a feast.

Get in on the planning. You and your patrol will be a lot more involved in camping if you're in on the planning. But when there's a planning session, roll up your sleeves, get serious, and show that you can make a business meeting work.

Go many places. The adventure goes out of a place if you go there too often. So does the challenge. Your patrol will be strengthened by many experiences — but not by the same one 10 times in a row.

Service Projects.—Patrols should blossom when the troop has a service project. Here are some ways to make sure that they do.

- The patrols themselves should be involved in the planning. They should have a voice in *how* to do it, but more importantly, *what's* to be done.
- The service project should be planned so that every patrol has a worthwhile part. Each patrol should do its part as a patrol.
- Patrols should review the project—and their part in it — after it is completed. They should evaluate how well the job was done, what good it did, and what they learned from it.
- Service projects should usually not last very long. Boys often lose interest in projects that stretch out over a long period.

Shows and Expositions.—As with other activities, patrols should have a voice in planning what the troop will do. Once that is decided, every patrol can have its part in getting ready for the big event.

Whenever possible, the troop's part in the show should be planned for patrol participation. This may amount only to each patrol having a period of time to operate a booth. However it is done, the troop's part in the show should strengthen the patrols.

In general, patrols are strengthened by having an important part in troop activities. They grow by taking assignments and carrying them out. The more chances they have, the better they become at getting the job done and keeping the group together. At the same time, they are proving to themselves and others that they can succeed as patrols. As they show that, patrols can do more on their own.

Courts of Honor.—Patrols should have a voice in planning every court of honor. On the big occasion, every patrol should have an important part. Patrols can be made responsible for printing programs, setting up the court of honor area, providing color guards and honor guards, and many other parts of the court of honor.

The Patrol On Its Own

The patrol grows up to the point that it can work away from the troop.

What does it mean to "work"?

The patrol "works" when — under its own leadership — it gets the job done and stays together.

Does that sound like leadership? It does, and it is. The patrol grows up under its leadership, or it doesn't grow up at all.

How long does it take for a patrol to be able to do things on its own? It depends. One patrol might do it in a few months. Another might take a year or more. Some patrols never make it.

Here are the kinds of things patrols can learn to do on their own.

Patrol Meetings.—A patrol can hold a meeting as a part of a troop meeting or at another time and place. There is no point in just having regular meetings often. But there is every reason to have a patrol

meeting to accomplish some patrol business.

This patrol business may grow out of the troop program. Often the patrol must plan or practice or organize itself for its part in troop activities. When there is such work to be done, the patrol meets to do it, as often as necessary.

Every patrol leader must learn to manage patrol meetings; not because there is some magic in having meetings, but because there is a job to do. The patrol leader must see that the job gets done and that the patrol stays together.

Let's take a simple example to see how a patrol meeting comes about.

The district is going to have a Scout exposition in a big armory. Thousands of people will attend. The troop leaders' council has decided that the troop will take part in a kind of three-ring circus in the main hall. Each patrol in the troop will choose an act, prepare it, and put it on.

The Jaguar Patrol will decide on its act during that part of the next troop meeting set aside for patrol meetings. The patrol leader writes down what he wants to get done. This simple device is called an *agenda*.

The patrol leader knows that once they choose an act, the patrol will have to meet to rehearse it. Selection is only the beginning.

The Jaguars decide to do a tumbling act. Mike Leonard is the best resource, because he has done a lot of tumbling. He is put in charge. They don't have much time in the troop meeting, but they try a couple of tumbling routines. The patrol is pretty bad. They decide to meet twice in the next week to practice. They pick times and places.

After two practices, the Jaguars decide they're not ready for the show. They decide to have two more practice sessions. None of their meetings has any other activity—just tumbling. They *could* do other things, but they agree not to. They work on getting the job done.

Here, then, is an example of the way a patrol can use meetings. The Jaguars have no regular meetings, but when they *need* them, they *have* them.

Patrol Hikes.—A patrol "hike" sounds like a 1-day thing and you go on foot. Actually, it could be almost anything that can be done by a patrol in a day: a bike hike, a horseback ride, a trip to the beach, or a walk to a local park or point of historical interest within the city. If you live near public parks or other good hiking territory, take advantage of them. But don't give up the idea of a patrol hike just because there's no great hiking area nearby.

A Scout patrol doesn't just start out to hike on its own. It will first need to prepare itself in skill and attitude. After all, permission has to be given by the Scoutmaster for patrol activities. In turn, each Scout has to get his parents' permission to go. Until all concerned know that the patrol can work on its own, permission will be hard to get.

The patrol hike is a true test of your patrol. Can you get the job done?—get to your destination?—have a great time?—

act like Scouts?—get home in good health and on time? Almost any patrol can do this with adults in charge. Can yours? If it can, isn't it the patrol leader who makes this possible? If it can't, perhaps you're not ready for this much leadership.

The aim of every patrol should be to do things on its own and do them well. The aim of every patrol leader should be to get his gang in shape to do that.

Patrol Advancement Projects.—We've mentioned that patrols work best when members share some common interests. These interests sometimes lead to similar concerns in advancement. Your patrol may get interested in a skill award or merit badge. And why shouldn't they work on them together if they want to?

Suppose everybody in the patrol is interested in the Conservation skill award. Your patrol meets with an instructor and learns what they have to do. Each member selects his own way of completing his projects. The patrol shares ideas. Everyone learns more than he would have alone.

There is probably no advancement project that could not be done as a patrol. Such projects are as natural as—well, a patrol hike.

Other Patrol Activities.—There is no end to what a patrol can do together. Here are a few more ideas, but the list could go on and on. Talk it over with the members of your patrol. They will come up with more ideas.

Visit a big airport.

Build a tree fort or a dam or a bridge.

Take golf lessons.

Plant trees.

Help an elderly couple keep house.

Improve the council's Scout camp.

Go fishing, skiing, canoeing, trapping.

Visit a museum.

Go to a ball game.

Visit sick children and put on a show.

Clean up a roadside or a creek bed.

Visit a factory or mine.

Collect rock samples.

Fix up the troop equipment or the place where it's stored.

Paint somebody's barn.

Raise money for a minipark.

Challenge another patrol to a game or contest.

Help in the school library.

The important thing about patrol activities is to have them. They can be mixtures of all sorts of things. Some can be for other people — service projects. Some can be trips. Some can be educational.

But do them. The patrol rises or falls on what it does. No patrol ever amounted to anything just standing there.

Patrol Spirit

Group spirit is hard to define. You can't see it or taste it, but you know when it's there.

When a patrol has spirit, you can tell by the way the Scouts walk and talk. Their smiles show it. Nobody says, "I'm glad I'm here," but you know they are. They also seem to be saying to each other, "I'm glad we're all here."

Every patrol has Scouts, uniforms, and a leader. But not every patrol has spirit. So it must take something more than that. But what? What gives a patrol spirit?

Are you ready for the magic word? It's *activity*. The things the patrol *does* — as a patrol — make spirit. Activities don't make spirit automatically, but you can't get spirit without them.

No, there's nothing special about the patrol that stands over here. Or meets in the corner over there. Or has this name instead of that name.

A patrol is special because it does things together. They have a ball. They get things done and know it. They work together. They're proud of themselves. They know they're good.

All of this can happen only if the patrol does things as a patrol. So the first — last — only prescription for patrol spirit is *activity*.

But as we noted, activity alone doesn't do it. The patrol really has to get somewhere, not just jump up and down in one place. And that's where the leader comes in. He sees to it that the job gets done. And that the patrol stays together. Out of this, comes spirit.

The following tips will help, but don't try to use them *instead* of activity. Use them *along with* activity:

- Get 'em whistling or singing while they work.
- Give lots of praise and not many threats.
- Be sure they accomplish something and know it.
- Smile.

- Help smooth over disagreements.
- Don't allow picking on somebody.

Know the Resources of Your Patrol

In the last chapter we noted "knowing the resources of the group" as a leadership skill. Now we can see how that skill can be used in leading a patrol.

Knowing Patrol Members.—Every member of every patrol is a resource. Each has the things he does best. Each has his special interests. Very often, these go together: What a fellow does well, he likes to do. Or the reverse: What he likes to do, he does well.

The patrol can make good use of its members' resources. To get any job done, any problem solved, the skills and interests of members can help. That is, they can if you know what they are.

How do you learn about these resources? There are only a couple of ways

1. *Ask.* Talk to your patrol members. Ask what they like to do. Ask what they do well. What sports or art or other group activities do they do? What are their hobbies? How do they spend their spare time?

2. *Watch.* The patrol in action exposes special skills and interests. Jim likes to teach first aid. Nick can climb a pole like a cat. When you hike through the woods, Pete sees things that everybody else misses. All of these individual skills and interests make the member especially valuable to the patrol. Another reason for knowing the re-

sources of the group: This will help you decide how much leadership you can share. Earlier in this chapter, a patrol leader put a member in charge of a tumbling act because he had experience. He shared leadership because he knew he could.

3. *Inquire of Others.* Your Scoutmaster has knowledge about every Scout in the troop through the personal growth agreement conferences. Talk to him about the interests and abilities of your patrol members.

You can keep track of the resources of your patrol members in your notebook or by keeping a simple card file like the one shown.

Knowing Your Equipment.—If your troop assigns equipment to patrols or if you check it out as you need it, you need to know just what it is, where it is, and what condition it's in. If something is missing or broken, you need to report that.

You should keep an inventory (list) of any equipment owned by your patrol. There is space for this in the *Patrol Record,* No. 3139. You should keep this list updated.

Your *Scout Handbook* and the *Camping* merit badge pamphlet have excellent ideas for troop and patrol equipment.

Understand, as patrol leader you do not have to be the patrol quartermaster. Somebody else can do that. But as patrol leader you must assign the job and see that it gets done.

Outside Resources.—There is no end to the resources available to the patrol.

Here are some samples of resources that you should know and be able to use:

- Fathers of Scouts — jobs, hobbies, skills, equipment
- Merit badge counselors
- School and public libraries
- Troop leaders and committee members
- Public parks and other places to go
- Maps

The Patrol Leader

This part deals with the patrol leader himself—how he gets his job, what he does, to whom he is responsible.

Qualifications. These are decided by the troop leaders' council and apply to all candidates for patrol leader within any one patrol, but may be different between patrols within a troop. They should be reasonable and in keeping with the patrol. For example, in a new patrol where the highest ranking Scout is a Tenderfoot, there is no point in saying that First Class is a qualification for patrol leader.

Here are examples of things that might be included in patrol leader qualifications. Each is followed by a recommendation, which may be accepted or not by your troop leaders' council.

- Age: 12 or 13
- Progress Award Earned: First Class or above
- School Grade: In keeping with age
- Membership in Patrol: 6-month minimum
- Experience in Patrol: Active participa-

tion in patrol and troop meetings and activities.

The troop leaders' council should review the qualifications at least once a year. Their objective should be to upgrade standards and to get them in line with or higher than the recommendations.

The patrol leader is elected by the members of the patrol. His recommended term of office is 6 months. He may be re-elected to office.

Duties. The patrol leader:

- Presides at all patrol events, meetings, and activities (unless he assigns the job to someone else).
- Represents the patrol on the troop leaders' council, of which he is automatically a member.
- Appoints an assistant patrol leader.
- Assigns duties and responsibilities to patrol members as needed.

The Patrol Leader Relates to His Patrol Members.—The patrol leader is first responsible to the members of the patrol. They elected him. They expect him to lead. This will require him to make decisions and to take action that will be in the best interest of the entire patrol.

The patrol has other leaders. The patrol leader appoints an assistant. He also appoints, as needed, other patrol members to carry out certain tasks.

The patrol leader may assign jobs to members of the patrol, as needed, such as the routine schedule for food preparation on an overnight camp. He makes sure they understand the job and sees that the assigned jobs are carried out.

DUTY ROSTER			
	CLEAN-UP	COOKING	FUEL AND WATER
FRI.	Jerry Ted	Mike Joe	Phil Gene
SAT.	Phil Gene	Jerry Ted	Mike Joe
SUN.	Mike Joe	Phil Gene	Paul Ted
MON.	Paul Ted	Mike Joe	Phil Gene
TUE.	Phil Gene	Paul Ted	Mike Jerry
WED.	Mike Jerry	Phil Gene	Paul Ted
THUR.	Paul Ted	Mike Joe	Phil Gene

DUTY ROSTER PLAN

Assign buddies to duties, but adjust assignments to share duties fairly among patrol members. Keep the system flexible to get things done—the job is the big thing. Assignments change daily after lunch cleanup.

Fuel and water buddies maintain water supply; maintain supplies of tinder, kindling, and firewood/charcoal and protect it from weather; and start fires in time for cooks to have meals ready on time.

Cooking buddies assemble food supplies; follow menus and recipes exactly; serve meals on time; put away food; put cook pots to soak; and have cleanup water supply on fire before serving meals.

Cleanup buddies set up wash and rinse water for dishwashing; clean cooking pots and utensils; clean kitchen and dining areas; store all group equipment; dispose of garbage and trash; and put out fire.

The Patrol Leader Relates to the Troop.— There is, in almost every troop, more than one patrol. The leaders of each patrol report to the senior patrol leader. He has the authority and the "command" position. There are other troop leaders who are "support" staff—the scribe, quartermaster, librarian, and instructors.

RELATIONSHIP TO THE SENIOR PATROL LEADER

Patrol Leader:	Senior Patrol Leader:
Responsible for the activity and actions of the patrol, an assembly of Scouts	Responsible for the activity and actions of the troop, an assembly of patrols
Assigns tasks and authority to Scouts within the patrol	Assigns tasks and authority to troop staff and, on mutual agreement with patrol leaders, to patrols
Attends troop leaders' council meetings, representing his patrol members	Plans and conducts meetings of troop leaders' council with Scoutmaster's help
Carries out programs and activities agreed upon by troop leaders' council, delegating tasks to patrol members as necessary	Carries out programs and activities agreed upon by troop leaders' council, delegating tasks to troop staff as necessary

Patrol Leader:	Senior Patrol Leader:
Plans and conducts meetings of the patrol	Conducts meetings of the troop as planned by the troop leaders' council
May ask for help of troop staff or leadership corps through senior patrol leader	May ask for services of patrol members as instructors or den chiefs through patrol leader
May participate as a member of Scout progress review for Tenderfoot, Second Class, or First Class upon assignment by senior patrol leader	Conducts and/or assigns authority to members of troop leaders' council or leadership corps to conduct Scout progress review for Tenderfoot, Second Class, and First Class

Relationship to Troop Staff.—The scribe, quartermaster, and librarian are appointed by the senior patrol leader to provide support services to the troop and its patrols. Patrol leaders will have contact with these troop officers and may request their services through the senior patrol leader as necessary.

As patrol leader, you will appoint members of your patrol to collect dues and record attendance, and they will file their reports with the troop scribe. Others may be assigned to check out equipment with the troop quartermaster.

Relationship to Assistant Senior Patrol Leader.—In larger troops, an assistant senior patrol leader may be appointed by the senior patrol leader. He will have specific areas of authority assigned to him such as the leadership corps, the Scout progress review, or training new patrol leaders. Your relationship with such a person, if there is one, will be the same as with the senior patrol leader.

Relationship to the Scoutmaster.—The Scoutmaster and his assistant(s) are responsible for all the actions and activities of the troop. The Scoutmaster is your counselor regarding program, patrol members, relationships with other members, and personal growth. You can always share any of your problems with him in confidence.

Likewise, your Scoutmaster is always looking for ideas and suggestions for the good of the troop. He wants to share your successes. He wants you and your patrol to feel successful and happy. Always feel free to consult him.

Chapter Five

THE LEADERSHIP
OF THE TROOP

HOW a troop's leadership is organized, selected, and carries out assignments is important. Have you ever considered how the leadership in your troop is organized? Who is responsible to carry out certain tasks and why?

Is it important for you to know who has authority to make decisions? Let's take a look at some troop leadership plans.

Troop Organization

There is no single way to organize a troop. The organizations shown here are samples only. Your troop can organize

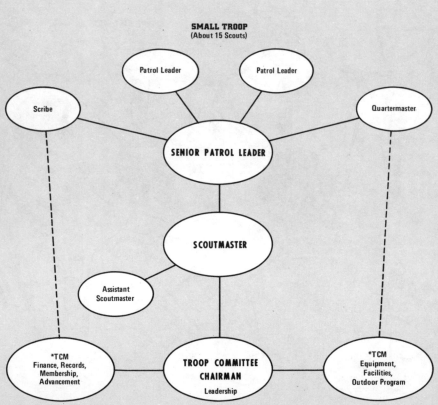

SMALL TROOP
(About 15 Scouts)

*TCM — Troop Committee Member

itself best. The larger it is, the more organization it will need and probably have.

You should not take any of this to mean that large troops are better than average or small ones. The best size troop is the one that delivers the best Scout program.

Here is an organization for a small troop (under 15 members). This one may only have been organized a few weeks. If it grows, as it probably will, it will need to change its organization.

Average size troops (30 members) need more organization. In order that the Scoutmaster is not tied down to every troop function, some jobs are delegated to

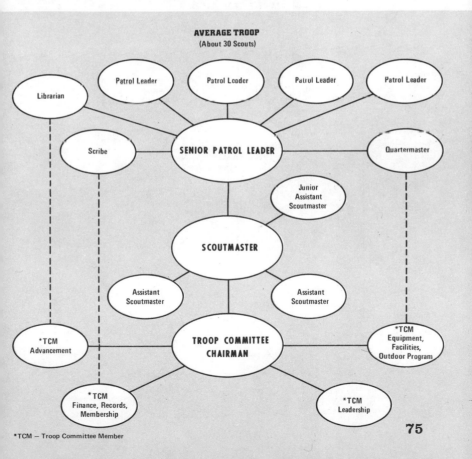

AVERAGE TROOP
(About 30 Scouts)

*TCM — Troop Committee Member

75

LARGE TROOP
(About 60 Scouts)

Patrol Leader

Patrol Leader

Patrol Leader

Patrol Leader

Patrol Leader

Patrol Leader

Patrol Leader

Assistant Senior Patrol Leader

Assistant Senior Patrol Leader

Librarian

Scribe

SENIOR PATROL LEADER

Leadership Corps Assistant Senior Patrol Leader

Quartermaster

Junior Assistant Scoutmaster

Junior Assistant Scoutmaster

SCOUTMASTER

Assistant Scoutmaster

Assistant Scoutmaster

*TCM Advancement

*TCM Finance, Records

TROOP COMMITTEE CHAIRMAN

*TCM Membership

*TCM Leadership

*TCM Outdoor Program

*TCM Equipment, Facilities

*TCM — Troop Committee Member

assistant Scoutmasters and troop committee members. You can see these jobs in the diagram below.

Some troops grow from 50 to over 100 members. Such large troops need even more organization than is shown in the last diagram. Troops with a leadership corps will have a slightly different organization (see page 121).

A troop organizes to meet its needs. The jobs to be done and the people to do them have to be matched.

The Troop's Adult Leaders

There are only two adult leader designations in a troop: the *Scoutmaster* and his *assistant Scoutmaster(s)*. There can be only one Scoutmaster per troop, of course. But a troop may have as many assistant Scoutmasters as it needs and can recruit.

What are the Scoutmaster's job and qualifications?

A *Scoutmaster* is:
• Appointed by the troop committee.
• Responsible to the troop committee.
• At least 21 years old.

He is responsible for:
• Managing the troop program.
• The actions of the troop leaders' council.
• The welfare of every Scout in troop and patrol activities.
• Training and coaching the other leaders.
• Showing a personal interest in every Scout and his development.

An assistant Scoutmaster takes over for the Scoutmaster in his absence, but that is not his main job.

An *assistant Scoutmaster* is:

- Appointed by the troop committee on the Scoutmaster's recommendation.
- At least 18 years old (every troop should have at least one assistant who is 21 or older who could replace the Scoutmaster if necessary).
- Responsible to the Scoutmaster. An assistant Scoutmaster shares leadership with the Scoutmaster according to his skills and interests and the needs of the troop. Here are common assignments for assistant Scoutmasters:

    Activities

    Physical arrangements

    Advancement

    Leadership corps

A junior assistant Scoutmaster is a young man who is well qualified to be an assistant Scoutmaster but is not yet old enough.

A *junior assistant Scoutmaster* is:

- Appointed by the Scoutmaster.
- Approved by the troop committee.
- Responsible to the Scoutmaster.
- 16 or 17 years old.

Like the assistant, the junior assistant Scoutmaster handles specific tasks that match the troop's needs and his skills and interests. Junior assistant Scoutmasters may do jobs like these:

Train Scoutcraft instructors. Show instructors how to put on effective demonstrations through the use of visual aids, including participation by the learners.

Coordinate campfires. Develops a list of resources for campfires such as song leaders, storytellers, Indian dancers, game leaders for troop meetings, camp-outs, and long-term camp.

Train den chiefs. Becomes acquainted with the Cub Scout program and leaders. Gives regular guidance to den chiefs in songs, games, and skills related to the "theme of the month."

Direct courts of honor. Takes over props, lighting, and other stagecraft.

Coordinate special events. Provides special services for hikes, camp-outs, vocational tours, historic hikes, and other events.

Supervise Order of the Arrow functions. Handles the election of new members, helps prepare for tap-outs and inductions with a local lodge, and oversees service projects of a troop and troop participation in local lodge activities.

The Troop's Elected Leader

The boy leader with the greatest responsibility in the troop is the senior patrol leader. He reports directly to the Scoutmaster.

Qualifications. The troop leaders' council develops these qualifications to fit the situation. Boys in a new troop are not likely to have progress awards, camping or leadership experience, so these should not be a requirement for this office. As the troop grows in size and experience, the qualifications should be revised. The following qualifications are recommended for an established troop:

- Age: 13 to 15
- Progress Award: First Class or higher
- School Grade: In keeping with age
- Time in Troop: 1-year minimum
- Leadership Experience in Troop: Have served as patrol leader or assistant senior patrol leader
- Camping Experience: Both long-term and short-term participation.

Elected by. All the Scouts in the troop.

Term of office. This is decided by the troop leaders' council. It is recommended that it not be less than 6 months.

Responsible to. The Scoutmaster.

Duties. The senior patrol leader:

- Presides at all troop meetings, events, and activities.
- Leads the troop leaders' council.
- Appoints assistant senior patrol leader with the Scoutmaster's counsel.
- Assigns duties and responsibilities to other leaders.
- Appoints a scribe, quartermaster, and librarian with the counsel of the Scoutmaster.

How the Senior Patrol Leader Relates to Others.—The senior patrol leader must learn how to cooperate with and relate to others.

To the Scoutmaster. The Scoutmaster helps in the development of the senior patrol leader by training, coaching, and counseling. They work closely together in every part of the troop program. The

Scoutmaster works through the senior patrol leader to keep the troop leaders' council informed of his goals and ideas with the possible exception of matters concerning discipline and safety.

To the assistant and junior assistant Scoutmasters. If an assistant Scoutmaster is substituting for the Scoutmaster, the SPL works with him the same as with the Scoutmaster.

When the Scoutmaster delegates part of his authority to an assistant Scoutmaster, he must make this clear to the senior patrol leader (SPL).

When the SPL has a question of authority, he asks the Scoutmaster.

Assistant Scoutmasters should not cut the line of authority from the SPL to the troop. Instead, they should work through the SPL.

There are obvious exceptions to this. For example, if a junior assistant Scoutmaster (JASM) is responsible to work with the leadership corps on a project, he simply does so. If an assistant Scoutmaster coaches the quartermaster, they just go at their work.

To the troop committee. The SPL does not work directly with the troop committee. If there is communication between them, it is through the Scoutmaster.

To assistant senior patrol leaders. He appoints one or more with the approval of the Scoutmaster. He then assigns their duties and they report to him. An assistant senior patrol leader (ASPL) serves in the SPL's absence.

To patrol leaders. The SPL trains and counsels them. He is their chairman in the troop leaders' council. They look to him for leadership at all troop functions.

To troop staff. This refers to the quartermaster, scribe, librarian, and instructors. The SPL appoints Scouts to fill these positions. They are trained and coached by troop committee members having related responsibilities. They report to the SPL, but they retain membership in a patrol or the leadership corps.

To the leadership corps. If the troop has a leadership corps, the SPL is its leader. (He may delegate this job to an ASPL.) He assigns their duties and counsels members of the corps as necessary. The corps' standards of operation and conduct come from the SPL.

To the troop members. Scouts in the troop should recognize the SPL as the highest boy leader in the troop. He should demonstrate the highest order of Scout spirit, conduct, and leadership. In turn, the SPL must have the highest regard for each Scout as an individual.

Appointed Leaders

In this part we consider six appointed boy leaders of the troop. All are appointed by the SPL with the counsel of the Scoutmaster. All are responsible to the SPL except den chiefs. The term of office of each is set by the SPL and need not be the same for all. Here are their duties.

Assistant Senior Patrol Leader

- Trains and guides patrol leaders.
- Gives troop meeting and activity leadership.

- Serves as chairman of the Scout progress review.
- Takes over for SPL in his absence.

Scribe
- Keeps a log of troop leaders' council decisions.
- Records attendance and dues payments.
- Records advancement in the troop records.

He may look to the Scoutmaster or a troop committee member with record responsibility for guidance.

Quartermaster
- Keeps records on patrol and troop equipment.
- Keeps equipment in good repair for instant use.
- Checks out equipment to patrols and sees that it is returned in good order.
- Suggests needed new or replacement equipment to the SPL or troop leaders' council.

He may look to the Scoutmaster or a troop committee member with property responsibility for guidance.

Librarian
- Keeps records on literature owned by the troop.
- Advises SPL or Scoutmaster of new or replacement items needed.
- Has literature available for borrowing at troop meetings.
- Keeps a system for checking literature in and out. Follows up on late returns.
- Keeps the merit badge counselor list.

He may look to the Scoutmaster or a troop committee member with advancement responsibility for guidance.

Instructor

- Instructs troop members in one or more skills for which he is qualified.

Den Chief

- The den chief is an appointed troop officer.
- He is the activities assistant in one den of a Cub pack.

In the troop, he is responsible to whatever leader is in charge of the den chief program. Meanwhile, as a Scout, he is a member of a patrol.

Den chiefs should not hold a second leadership office in the troop. For example, being both a den chief and a patrol leader may require more time than most Scouts can give.

The den chief may be trained for his work by the Cub pack or by the den chief coordinator (JASM or leadership corps). His week-to-week responsibilities in the den are assigned by the den leader. His example encourages younger boys to become Scouts.

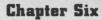

Chapter Six

HOW THE TROOP WORKS

II N earlier chapters, this handbook considers leadership and individual leaders. In this chapter we will see how leaders work together as a team to make the troop successful. We will take up the troop leaders' council and its meetings. We will look at troop meetings, the Scout progress review, and the need for recordkeeping.

By now you have learned that activity is what holds patrols and the troop together. Here you will see how a team of leaders works together to carry on activities.

We'll begin by looking closely at the troop leaders' council.

The Troop Leaders' Council

The troop leaders' council operates the troop. Every Scout is represented on the

THE TROOP LEADERS' COUNCIL

PATROL LEADER   PATROL LEADER   PATROL LEADER   PATROL LEADER

SCOUTMASTER
COUNSELOR

SENIOR PATROL LEADER
CHAIRMAN

council by a leader. Patrol members are represented by their patrol leaders. Troops with a leadership corps may have that body represented by the assistant senior patrol leader.

The troop leaders' council plans the troop program and then carries it out. It also has other important functions, as you will soon see.

The diagram shows the membership of a typical troop leaders' council. The members shown are the only ones who have a vote. The number of members changes only if there are more or fewer patrols.

Is the librarian a member?

Does the Scoutmaster have a vote?

What adult leaders are members of the council?

As you can see, no members of the troop staff are members of the troop leaders' council. (An exception is when the leadership corps is led and represented by an assistant senior patrol leader.) No adult leader is a member of the council.

The Scoutmaster serves as the adult counselor to the troop leaders' council. He has no vote.

Troop leaders who are not members of the troop leaders' council may attend meetings if invited. They have no vote and should not be allowed in such large numbers that they dominate the meetings.

The troop leaders' council has the following responsibilities:

• Planning the troop program.
• Making the program happen.
• Conducting the Scout progress review.
• Dealing with patrol problems.

It carries out these jobs under the leadership of the senior patrol leader. In turn, he is counselled and coached by the Scoutmaster.

You should understand the difference between what the troop leaders' council does and what the troop committee does.

The troop leaders' council is directly involved in planning and operating the week-to-week troop program. It is boy leaders, working directly with boys and boy program.

The troop committee, on the other hand, supports the troop with certain services that are not supplied by the adult leaders. These include supervising the troop's budget, finding places to camp, recruiting good adult leaders, and other such jobs. The troop committee does not do much dealing directly with the Scouts and is not directly involved in regular troop program. They sometimes assist at special activities and give guidance to some members of the troop staff.

Meetings of the Troop Leaders' Council

The troop leaders' council has four types of meetings:
- Annual planning conference
- Monthly planning meeting
- Brief meetings after each troop meeting
- Special meetings

The Annual Planning Conference.—This annual effort of the troop leadership team should be entered into with enthusiasm and plenty of advanced preparation.

Objectives. Plan the troop program in outline for 12 months and train the troop leadership team.

Where and When. When you have the annual planning conference depends on your troop's program year. For example, many troops use the year beginning in September and ending the following August. Such troops do their annual planning during the summer.

Whatever your troop's program year, the annual planning should be done a month or more before that year begins.

Where you have it depends on the amount of time you devote to it. Some troops do their annual planning in a single evening and do the training on other occasions. Others spend a whole day or weekend in planning for the year and training leaders. For a short meeting, the troop

meeting place or someone's home is fine.
For a day or a weekend, a camp, farm, or
someone's summer cottage makes a great
place.

Preparation. Troop and patrol leaders
have some things to do in advance of the
conference.

The senior patrol leader and Scoutmaster should:

- Study *Scouting Program Helps.*
- Determine the troop's program year.
- Make entries on the Troop Annual
  Planning Worksheet:
  Important community event dates in-
  cluding school, religious, and civic holi-
  days and activities
  Dates for troop committee meetings
  and district roundtables
  District and council activity dates
  Court of honor dates

Patrol leaders should ask their Scouts
for ideas and suggestions for the troop
program. Review last year's activities and
note those they would like to repeat. Make
a list of new program features they would
like and bring it to the planning conference. This is how you represent your
patrol at the annual conference.

The troop staff should prepare physical
arrangements and morale activities for
the conference. They can call on an assistant Scoutmaster or other adult for help.

Content of the Conference (more details
on pages 117-18).

- Statement of purpose by Scoutmaster
- Reports on ideas and suggestions from
  patrol leaders

- Introduction of *Scouting Program Helps* by senior patrol leader
- Selection of special events for the year, including major service projects, tours, overnight camps, hikes, long-term camp, Scout show, rallies, etc. Select dates for each.
- Selection of program features that can help the troop prepare for its special events. Schedule them.
- Completion of the calendar by filling in "open dates" with short-term activities; determine monthly planning meeting dates for the troop leaders' council; make assignments for further program development of major events.

Monthly Planning Meeting.—This is a monthly meeting to check on progress to date.

Objectives. Plan details of next month's troop program and assign responsibilities for that program.

When and Where. This planning meeting should be held sometime during the month *ahead* of the monthly program being planned. The troop meeting place or someone's home is the usual meeting place. This meeting is held in the evening or on a weekend and lasts from 1 to 2 hours.

Some troops hold this monthly meeting on the same night as troop meetings—but no troop meeting is held that night. For example, a troop may meet on the first, second, and third Monday of the month. The troop leaders' council meets on the fourth Monday, usually following a weekend special event for the entire troop.

Preparation. Your Scoutmaster attends the monthly district roundtable for ideas. He then notes any ideas for troop meetings on copies of the Troop Meeting Plan sheet, No. 4425.

Both the senior patrol leader and the Scoutmaster should:

- Review the Troop Annual Planning Worksheet for the next month.
- Review the suggested sources for program helps for the month.
- Evaluate progress on the year-round programs.
- Meet to plan and write out the agenda for the troop leaders' council meeting.

Content of the Monthly Planning Meeting (more details on pages 119-20).

- Read "Log of Decisions" from last meeting and evaluate progress.
- Patrol leader reports.
- Scout progress review candidates for Star, Life, or Eagle to be considered for recommendation to the troop committee.
- Discussion on year-round projects or unfinished business.
- Planning details for next month: special events, troop meetings, patrol meetings or activities.
- Refresher session in games, ceremonies, or skills scheduled into this month's program.
- Scoutmaster's minute.

Brief Meeting After the Troop Meeting.— This is an on-the-spot review meeting for leaders.

Objectives. Evaluate the meeting; check on the details and assignments for the next meeting.

Preparation. The Scoutmaster should tell the SPL anything he wants brought up at this brief meeting. It is best for the Scoutmaster to be able to talk to individual Scouts after the troop meeting, so the senior patrol leader should be able to run the troop leaders' council meeting without the Scoutmaster being present.

The senior patrol leader should make notes during the troop meeting on any parts of the meeting he wants to discuss. He should also review the Troop Meeting Plan Sheet for the next meeting so he knows what needs to be brought up.

Content of Meeting. Make sure these points are covered:

- Brief evaluation of the troop meeting. Discuss anything that went wrong to avoid making the same mistake again. Praise those who came prepared and did a good job.
- Brief review of next meeting or activity and assignments given earlier. Make changes if necessary.
- Patrol leaders may submit names of Scouts ready for Scout progress review.

Special Meetings.—The senior patrol leader may call a special meeting of the troop leaders' council whenever one is needed. Examples might be:

- To evaluate plans and check details for some big activity—such as summer camp.
- To solve problems—such as a group behavior problem at camp or camporee.

- To meet emergency conditions—to put a "Plan B" or alternate plan into effect because of bad weather, vehicle breakdown, or other emergency.

Such special meetings are not necessarily long and may deal with only one subject. Sometimes, no advance planning or notice is possible. A need arises, and the senior patrol leader meets it by calling a special meeting.

It is important that the troop leaders' council meet and deal with special situations. For the Scoutmaster or other leaders to take over is to weaken the troop leaders' council. Naturally, a meeting can't be called for every little problem. But when the troop leaders' council can be called on to handle things, it should be.

Troop Meetings

The objectives of troop meetings are:
- To provide opportunities to practice the patrol method.
- To give each Scout a chance to learn and to complete skill requirements.
- To promote patrol spirit through individual and patrol competition.
- To motivate Scouts by working with others, ceremonies, Scoutmaster's minutes, courts of honor, and other special events.
- To offer opportunities to lead.

The Parts of a Troop Meeting.—A good meeting should include the following eight parts.

Preopening: An activity in which everybody may join as they arrive. It begins when the first Scout arrives at the meeting and ends when the meeting is called to order. The point is to give Scouts something to do until the meeting begins.

Opening: A formal start to the meeting such as a ceremony, song, or uniform inspection.

Skill instruction or demonstration: An occasion for learning. It may involve the whole troop or be divided into interest groups.

Game or contest: An active everybody-takes-part affair. It may or may not involve one or more Scout skills. A game such as "skunk tag" is just for fun and involves no practice of a useful skill. A water-boiling contest involves the use of skills of wood preparation, fire building, cleanup, and teamwork. Both kinds of games are valuable in meetings, and both are fun.

Patrol Meeting: Held to conduct any necessary patrol business or preparation. Examples: Plan last-minute details for the hike, plan a menu, organize for a contest coming up next in the meeting. Patrol meetings must have a purpose; there must be things for the patrols to do.

Interpatrol Activity: Games, contests, demonstrations, or projects involving patrols as teams—often in competition.

Closing: The official completion of the meeting. May include announcements, recognition of Scouts' earning awards or new troop leadership positions, the Scoutmaster's minute, and a brief ceremony.

After the Meeting: Equipment is stored; room put in order. Troop leaders' council meets to plan details for next meeting.

Resources for Help.—Scouts usually attend more troop meetings than any other kind of get-together. There may be 40 or 50 troop meetings a year, though a troop can make do with fewer than that. But a large number of meetings means two things: (1) Planning interesting meetings is a big job, just because there are so many of them, and (2) Scouts are more likely to be bored by troop meetings than by anything else the troop does.

So you need to know your resources. What's available to help your troop have sparkling, fun-filled, constructive meetings? Here are some suggestions.

Manpower: Your troop is not limited to its Scouts, troop leaders, and Scoutmaster. Members of the troop committee, fathers of Scouts, and members of the sponsoring institution can all contribute to meetings. So can outside specialists such as the lieutenant from the police department, the fire marshal, the power squadron commander, the ski patrol member, the forester. Merit badge counselors will share their specialties with the troop. No matter where you live, there are people nearby who will help enliven your program.

Literature: The Boy Scouts of America publishes a lot of great materials to spice up your program with ideas. Here are the main ones:

For Patrol and Troop Leaders (Scouts):
- *Scout Handbook*
- *Fieldbook*
- *Boys' Life* magazine

- *Scouting Program Helps*
- Merit badge pamphlets
- *Patrol and Troop Activities*
- *Scout Songbook*
- *Troop Leader's Program Notebook*
  For Adult Leaders:
- *Scoutmaster's Handbook*
- *Scouting Magazine*
- Literature listed above for Scouts
- Troop Meeting Plan (a form)

Equipment: It is pretty hard to have a good meeting empty handed. If you're going to tie knots, you need rope. If you're going to practice tent pitching, you need some ground and some tents. Much of this, of course, comes right out of the troop supply closet. But there's no rule book that says you can't have a canoe demonstration, a boxing match, or a ski lesson. The troop meeting may have to be held somewhere else, and why not? If you can't borrow the equipment to come to you, go where it is. Have an occasional meeting in a swimming pool or skating rink. Every effort should be made to make troop meetings interesting and exciting by having the Scouts work with real equipment—not just talk about it or listen to talk about it. Imagination in getting and using equipment will go a long way toward making a troop meeting interesting.

Visual Aids: One of the best ways to demonstrate some things is with pictures. Learners can see and understand better if skills like artificial respiration or axmanship are illustrated in filmstrips or slides. Your council office probably has some such materials available for borrowing. There are some inexpensive skill materials you can buy. Just be sure that you are using film, slides, etc., to teach and not just to kill time. A cartoon about a cat chasing a mouse is not worth your time at a troop meeting. A film that demonstrates some conservation activities you can do might be worth a mint.

The Scout Progress Review for Tenderfoot, Second Class, and First Class

When a Scout has completed all requirements for a progress award, his work must be reviewed. In the case of the Tenderfoot, Second Class, and First Class progress awards, the review is handled by the troop leaders' council. The review has three purposes:

* To make sure the Scout has done what he was supposed to do for the progress award.
* To see how good an experience the Scout is having in the troop.
* To encourage the Scout to progress further.

Scheduling.—One plan is for the troop leaders' council to announce that Scout progress reviews will be held regularly on a given date. Your review might be every first Monday, or every third Thursday, or something like that. When that date comes, you review every Scout who is ready. Those who are not ready for review will know that the next review is only a month away.

Your troop leaders' council can also schedule reviews "as needed" but this means special meetings, and they are a little more difficult to get into everyone's schedule and may upset other plans.

Who Serves?—In larger troops, not all patrol leaders can sit in on every review. There would be just too many reviewers for each Scout. So patrol leaders take turns serving as members of the Scout progress review, making sure that everyone has a chance to serve.

In some troops, the duties of the patrol leaders may make it hard for them to serve in addition on the Scout progress review. In such instances, the senior patrol leader may assign the duty to troop leaders or to the leadership corps.

A reviewing group should have no less than three nor more than five members. When making assignments, alternates should be picked in case of last-minute absences.

The senior patrol leader is responsible for the reviewing function. He may delegate the task to an assistant senior patrol leader. Either the senior patrol leader or his assistant serves as chairman of the Scout progress review.

Your troop committee should assign one member to counsel the members of the Scout progress review. He will help you get organized, run good reviews, and accomplish your purpose. You should not expect him to run the review for you, however. That's your job.

The Setting for the Review.—Many troops hold reviews on troop meeting night,

separately from the meeting. If you can, use a quiet room where you can talk without being disturbed. You will need three or more chairs for the members of the Scout progress review and one for the candidate to be reviewed. (If more than one is to be reviewed, take them one at a time.) You may need a table to hold books and papers.

Before the Review.—Make a schedule of those who will appear to be reviewed.

To see how this happens, we'll take one example.

A Scout has completed all of the performance requirements for Tenderfoot. His patrol leader has "signed off" in his *Scout Progress Record*. His next step is to make an appointment with the Scoutmaster for a personal growth agreement conference.

When the conference is completed, the Scout tells his patrol leader that he's ready for the Scout progress review. The next time the troop leaders' council meets, the patrol leader tells the senior patrol leader that his patrol has a Tenderfoot candidate to be reviewed. The council will discuss the candidate briefly with the Scoutmaster and patrol leader. Remember that you are reviewing individuals. Any special items that should be brought out in the review can be brought up by the candidate's patrol leader at this time.

Getting Started.—The patrol leader presents any candidate from his patrol. A troop leader is presented to the Scout progress review by the senior patrol leader. If the candidate is the senior patrol leader himself, he is presented by the Scoutmaster. "Presented" means that the candidate's leader introduces the Scout to the Scout progress review, in the following manner:

"This is Scout Jack Kirner, a member of the Beagle Patrol. He is a candidate for Second Class. He has completed all the requirements, his scorebook is complete, and he has had a personal growth agreement conference with the Scoutmaster."

The review chairman would introduce the candidate to any members of the review team whom he doesn't already know. (In a large troop there might be some.)

The Scout candidate presents his records and is invited to sit down.

A few early questions are asked to relax the Scout, not to gather any useful information. You might ask when he joined the troop, what grade he's in, or about his hobbies or other interests. You need to make special efforts to be friendly and relaxed so that he will not feel threatened by the review.

The Review Itself.—The review is not an examination. An *examination* goes like this: "Jump in water over your head, swim 25 yards, turn about, etc...." A *review* of the same thing would be to respond to questions like these: "Where did you pass your Swimming skill award?" "Who tested you?" "What did he have you do?"

In other words, the Scout reviews what he did for his progress award. From his review, you are able to decide whether he did what he was supposed to. You also find out what kind of experience he is having in the troop. With that knowledge, you can better shape the troop program to meet most Scouts' needs and interests.

There is no standard set of questions that you should use. The review would come to have no meaning if you did use such questions. The object of the questions is to get the Scout to talk about his experiences in advancing. No one group of questions is just right for doing that. Here, however, are some samples of the kinds of questions you may ask:

- What did you do for the Citizenship skill award?
- Who passed you on the tests?
- Why did you choose that skill award? (Similar questions may be used about merit badges earned.)
- How is your attendance record for meetings? camp-outs? hikes? paper drives?
- What do you do in your life that shows the Scout Oath and Law at work?
- What is a good turn? What good turns have you done lately?
- What plans do you have for further advancement?
- What did you find easiest about working for this progress award? What was hardest?

The review does not consist just in asking questions. During the review, you, as a member of the Scout progress review, must form a judgment. You use his review as the basis for your judgment. Has he done the things that are required? What kind of experience is he having in the troop? Is he ready for advancement? Does he plan to go on from here?

Words of Warning.—The progress review can be a very useful experience for boys on both sides of the table. But you have to do it right. For instance:

Review just one Scout at a time. Each is entitled to his own review. Resist the idea of bunching up to save time.

Keep personal feelings out. The question is not whether you like the boy. The question is whether he has met the requirements. Don't pass him because you like him or fail him because you don't.

Do a good job. If you just run through the motions without really working at it, everyone will soon know the review is a joke. Scouts will be serious about advancement only if the review is serious.

The Scout is an applicant for an award. There is no call to embarrass, irritate, or otherwise treat him with anything less than respect.

Allow members of the review to disqualify themselves if they wish. If Fred wants to be excused from reviewing Johnny because they are close buddies, excuse him. (Plan ahead for situations like this.)

The Decision.—The review should last perhaps from 10 to 20 minutes. In that time, members of the Scout progress review can form an opinion as to whether the Scout is qualified to advance. You cannot ask about everything the Scout has done for the progress award, but you will be able to find out enough to make a judgment.

The Scout is asked to leave the room while the members of the Scout progress review discuss him. This should not take long. Usually, you will all agree either that he is or is not qualified.

The progress award will mean less to everyone if it is awarded to a poorly qualified Scout. Be sure in your own mind that you are not "shrinking" the badge by approving someone who hasn't really earned it. "Getting by" with shoddy work is not in the best interest of the Scout either. It will just encourage him to do more shoddy work.

If the members are satisfied that the Scout is ready to advance, he is called in and told that. Tell him that his badge will be presented at the next troop meeting.

If the members feel that the Scout is not ready to advance, he should be called in and told what he has done satisfactorily. On weak areas, he should be asked whether he has done his best. Most Scouts will readily admit that they have not and will accept responsibility for completing the requirements properly. If a Scout is not

so ready to admit poor preparation, the members of the review should point out the weaknesses and direct him to complete his work properly. Be very specific about what must be done.

When members of the progress review disagree about whether or not a candidate qualifies, it's the responsibility of the senior patrol leader to bring about a group decision. He may call upon the adult adviser for his counsel. This must be done before the candidate is called back.

You should tell the Scoutmaster, after the progress review is complete, of all decisions you made.

For the Record.—Whenever a Scout is approved for a progress award, the fact must be reported to your local council office. A special form is provided for that purpose. The senior patrol leader must be sure that all approved Scouts are entered on such a report.

He then gets the report to the advancement troop committee member, who will get it to the local council office. The Scout's record is not official unless it is recorded there.

Scout Progress Review for Star, Life, and Eagle

The troop leaders' council reviews scorebooks, but not the applicants themselves, for Star, Life, and Eagle progress award. If the troop leaders' council approves the applicant, he may be reviewed by the troop committee's progress review. If not, he is advised what additional preparation is needed.

No report need be filed by the troop leaders' council for Star, Life, and Eagle progress award. Such a report will be filed by the troop committee with the local council for successful Star, Life, and Eagle candidates.

Recordkeeping

The scribe, quartermaster, and librarian share the responsibility for troop records. Each has his own set of records to keep. We'll take up each set separately.

Troop Leaders' Council Meeting - March 22
Attendance: Present - Hughes, Roncotti, Flaherty, Jackson,
        Swenson, and Mr. Anderson
        Absent - Philips, Gross, and Mr. Richards

1. Meeting conducted by Dick Hughes senior patrol leader.
2. Flaherty reported that the Beavers would like permission to develop a special project to collect food and clothing for the Petersons, whose trailer house burned down last Monday. Project approved and other patrols agreed to follow Beavers' plan to be made at next week's troop meeting.
3. Roncotti reported that Smith and Miles were ready to meet with the progress review board for Second Class.
4. Jackson reported that Randy Michael had not been to meetings for 3 weeks and asked Mr. Anderson to please check up. Also Joe Weeks is ready for First Class project review.
5. The scribe gave each patrol leader a list of members behind on dues and asked them to pay up now. Mr. Anderson told us how to talk to Scouts who where behind on dues.
6. Senior patrol leader said Mr. Richards would have news about summer camp and all patrols should begin making plans on menus this month.
7. Plans for April program to prepare for district camporee to be held at Donner's Pond on May 16 and 17 (See Troop Meeting Plans attached for details)
8 Senior patrol leader appointed Flaherty and Philips to serve as members of the Scout progress review this month. Jackson is the alternate.

                Reported by
                Sam Swenson, troop scribe.

The troop scribe keeps these records as a minimum:

Troop leaders' council log of decisions
Attendance
Advancement
Dues and other funds

The Log of Decisions.—The troop leaders' council makes certain decisions when it meets. Some record must be made of these, and the scribe is the one who makes it. A simple composition notebook is OK for this purpose.

The log of decisions states in simple terms what was decided. On the opposite page is a sample from such a log.

At each meeting of the troop leaders' council, the log should be reviewed and any necessary action taken.

Records of the Scribe.—The troop scribe keeps a single set of records of attendance, dues, and advancement. Two recordkeeping tools are available from your Scout council office for this purpose. You should select the one you want to use, get it, and stick with it.

One basic tool is the *Troop Record Book*, No. 6509. This is looseleaf-notebook size, three-hole punched, and will accommodate the records of 40 Scouts in one copy. A new book must be started once a year, and additional books must be used when the membership of the troop goes above 40.

The other type of record is on individual sheets, one for each Scout. The Individual Scout Record, No. 6518, will hold a 3-year record for each Scout. These records are kept in a three-ring binder and separated by patrol. As members come and go, sheets may be added or removed.

Starting basic records. To get such a record going, you will need a copy of your troop's last charter application, plus applications of all members that they presented when joining. These two sources contain all the information you need to set up the original record. Other troop records will have to be consulted to get such information as advancement, merit badges, and troop offices held.

Adding and deleting records. When a new Scout joins the troop, his application should come to you. You record the information from it and pass it on to the Scoutmaster. If you are using the *Troop Record Book,* you add a line for the new Scout. If you are using the one-sheet records, you make out a new sheet for the new Scout.

When a Scout leaves the troop, you pencil out his line in the *Troop Record Book.* If using the individual record sheets, you just move his page to the "inactive" or "former Scout" part of your binder. Never destroy the old record.

Keeping attendance and dues records. At the beginning of each month you prepare a monthly dues envelope for each patrol. You put on the name of the patrol, list the members on the front, and put the dues status of each on it. For example, if Schmidt were behind 20 cents on his dues, you would write "-.20" after his name on the envelope.

A patrol member gets the envelope from you and records the information on the front about dues and attendance. He puts the money in the envelope that is paid in as dues. Then you get it back: envelope, record, and money.

You empty the money out, count it, make sure it tallies with the amount shown on the front, and put it in *your* envelope, Weekly Report to Treasurer, No. 3851. You record on the face of that envelope the amount received from each patrol.

You record the dues and attendance information from each patrol in your troop records. Then you return the envelopes to the patrols for reuse at the following meeting.

At the end of the month, you turn over all used patrol dues envelopes to the troop treasurer. Weekly, you turn over the dues money and any other money paid you by Scouts that is owed to the troop.

(The patrol can keep its own records, too, by using the *Patrol Record Book*, No. 6510.)

Keeping advancement records. Merit badges are earned one at a time and may be reported to the troop at any time when the Scout brings in his signed merit badge application. Each application should go through you first so that you can record the date that the merit badge was earned on the Scout's record.

Progress awards are finally approved by the Scout progress review conducted by the troop leaders' council or, in the case of Star, Life, and Eagle, by the troop committee. Both reviewing groups must file the Advancement Report, No. 4403, indicating successful candidates, with your council office. A copy of this report should be given to you to record this information in the *Troop Record Book* or the Individual Scout Record sheet, whichever your troop prefers.

The Scout's official advancement record (as well as attendance and dues) is the one kept by you. But it is kept neatly in a book, and few people see it. Advancement should also be kept where everyone can see progress. For this purpose, use the Troop Advancement Chart, No. 6506, and keep it updated. Whenever you post an advancement or a merit badge to troop records, post it also to the wall chart.

Forms to keep. As troop scribe, you will also have to keep supplies of forms that Scouts may need. These will include Application To Join a Scout Troop, No. 28-209; Patrol Dues Envelope, No. 3816; Weekly Report to Treasurer Envelope, No. 3851; and Inspection Report, No. 70-006.

Records Kept by the Librarian.—Most of the literature kept by the librarian is for use in advancement. Perhaps the most important of this literature is merit badge pamphlets.

Two big questions face a Scout who wants to work on a merit badge. One is "Where do I get the pamphlet?" The other is "Who are the counselors for this badge?" The librarian is able to answer both.

The librarian should be responsible for keeping an updated library of current merit badge pamphlets — not for all subjects, but for the most popular ones, at least. He keeps track of these with a card such as that shown on page 114.

The librarian also keeps an updated copy (or more than one) of the merit badge counselor list. When a Scout wants to get a merit badge, he should come to you for merit badge applications, which you will supply, and which the Scoutmaster must sign before the Scout sees the counselor.

Then when a Scout returns with a completed merit badge application, the librarian records it on the Troop Advancement Chart.

Records Kept by the Quartermaster.— The troop quartermaster is personally responsible for perhaps hundreds or even thousands of dollars' worth of troop equipment. It is not enough just to store all this gear neatly in some closet. There are two things that the quartermaster must be able to tell at all times: (1) just what the troop owns and (2) where it is.

To know what the troop owns, there must be an *inventory* of it. An inventory is a complete list of everything the troop owns. This should be recorded in your *Troop Financial Record Book*, No. 6508. A complete inventory should be made of all troop property at least once a year. Then when any item is added or removed, the list should be corrected.

With such a list, the quartermaster can match what he *should* have with what he *does* have. If the inventory shows that the troop owns four patrol cook kits, he should be able to find those cook kits. If there are two flagpoles on the inventory, there should be two in the closet. If there are two code buzzers in the closet, they should also be on the list.

You can see that the quartermaster is up against a hopeless job unless he has a checkout system. This is the other half of his records. The system shows that on

October 4 Sam Calmer took one patrol cook kit home. When Sam brings it back the quartermaster checks the condition of the equipment and logs that and the date on a file card for that item. This is the only way that the quartermaster can have any control over the equipment. Without such records, he has no idea what the troop owns or who has it. He must have absolute control over the equipment. If anyone else shares it, no system will work.

It takes some time and ingenuity to set up an inventory and checkout system for the troop's equipment. Shown below is a sample 4- by 6-inch card developed for troop inventory control and checkout. One card must be made for each item the troop owns. For instance, if the troop has four patrol cook kits, there should be four cards in the file on patrol cook kits.

FIRST AID MERIT BADGE PAMPHLET
Cost: $.45
Supplier: Brown's Dept. Store

Inventory
January 1971
January 1972

Checked Out	Name	Date Ret'd	Checked Out	Name	Date Ret'd

TRAIL CHEF COOK KIT (No. 1049)
Replacement Cost: $15.95
Supplier: Brown's Dept. Store

Troop Inventory
October 1971
January 1972

Check Out			Check In		
Date	Signature	Condition	Date	Condition	Accepted By

Chapter Seven

PLANNING MEETINGS
OF THE
TROOP LEADERS' COUNCIL

I N detail, here are sample agendas that your troop leaders' council may wish to use as a pattern in developing your own annual planning conference and monthly troop leaders' council meeting. These are suggestions; make your plans to fit your situation.

The Annual Planning Conference

Objectives

- To plan the troop program for 12 months
- To train patrol and troop leaders in Scoutcraft and leadership skills
- To provide recognition and morale building

Agenda

1. Preliminary items

- Senior patrol leader calls meeting to order and welcomes participants.
- Scoutmaster states the purpose of the meeting.
- Senior patrol leader gives an outline of how the conference will work and the schedule that will be followed.

2. Planning steps

- Report patrol members' suggestions on chalkboard or large sheets of paper. **Patrol leaders**

- Introduce *Scouting Program Helps*, identifying, where possible, items mentioned by patrol leaders in their reports. **Assistant senior patrol leader or assistant Scoutmaster**

- Break: Play a new game. **Junior assistant Scoutmaster**

- Review list of council and district events for the 12 months. Decide which ones troop will participate in. Enter those chosen on worksheet found in *Scouting Program Helps*. **Senior patrol leader**

- Select best program features from *Scouting Program Helps* that will prepare troop for the special events selected. Plot on calendar far enough ahead to allow preparation. **Senior patrol leader**

- Break: Prepare a meal. Sing some songs after meal. **Assistant Scoutmaster**
- Review special events chosen. Select additional special events for open months. Review Scouts' suggestion lists before choosing. **Senior patrol leader**
- Review additional special events and select the most appropriate special features to precede them. Plot them on the calendar. **Senior patrol leader**
- Break: Morale features. **Scoutmaster**
- Complete calendar by filling in short-term activities. **Senior patrol leader**
- Schedule regular monthly meetings of the troop leaders' council. **Senior patrol leader**
- Make assignments for further program development of major events such as long-term camp or service projects. **Senior patrol leader**
3. Other items that could be considered
- Equipment needed
- Budget building
- Patrol leader training

The Monthly Troop Leaders Council Meeting

Objectives

- To plan troop meetings and activities for the next month in detail.
- To make assignments to patrol and troop leaders.
- To refresh patrol leaders in skills to be used in next month's activities.

Agenda

1. Call to order.	**Senior patrol leader**
2. Review "Log of Decisions" from last month.	**Scribe**
3. Consider uncompleted projects from last month.	**Senior patrol leader**
4. Patrol reports on progress awards, activities, or problems.	**Patrol leaders**
5. Consider candidates for Star, Life, and Eagle progress review.	**Senior patrol leader/assistant senior patrol leader**
6. The Planning Steps	
• Review plan for the month made at annual planning conference.	**Senior patrol leader**
• New calendar developments and special program resources to be considered	**Scoutmaster**
• Progress on year-round programs to date	**Assistant Scoutmaster**
• Decide skills for emphasis in the month being planned.	**Senior patrol leader**
• Plan special event for the month and make assignments.	**Senior patrol leader**
• Plan troop and patrol meetings to prepare for special event and increase	**Senior patrol leader**

learning in selected skills. Make assignments to patrol and troop leaders.

NOTE: If assignments are made outside the troop leaders' council, be sure someone is responsible to make contact and to offer help.

- Review skills, techniques, and learning methods related to the month's program.

Junior assistant Scoutmaster/ leadership corps

7. Assignments for the month

Senior patrol leader

- Service patrol
- Program patrol
- Scout progress review

8. Announcements

Senior patrol leader

9. Scoutmaster's minute

Scoutmaster

| NO. 4417 350M 11-71 | **ADVANCEMENT REPORT** (PACK-TROOP-SHIP) BOY SCOUTS OF AMERICA | FOR COUNCIL OFFICE USE ONLY |

ADVANCEMENT REPORT
(PACK-TROOP-SHIP)
BOY SCOUTS OF AMERICA

NO. _____ DISTRICT _____

(PACK, TROOP, OR SHIP)

LEADER _____ ADDRESS _____

CITY _____ STATE _____ ZIP _____

EXPIRATION DATE OF UNIT _____ DATE AWARDS NEEDED _____

DATE THIS REPORT FORWARDED TO COUNCIL OFFICE _____

FOR COUNCIL OFFICE USE ONLY

REPORT RECEIVED _____

CERTIFICATES ISSUED _____

SCOREBOARDS ISSUED _____

MAILED OR ISSUED TO _____

DATE MAILED _____

RECORD POSTED _____

INSTRUCTIONS

1. Advancement procedures:

   Packs — When the Cubmaster receives a Den Advancement Report, No. 3847, from his den leaders, he then completes an Advancement Report for the entire pack. This Advancement Report must be signed by the Cubmaster and sent to the council office at least one week before a pack meeting.

   Troops — All Boy Scouts ready for advancement must appear personally before a board of review composed of at least three adult male citizens, preferably troop committee members. An Advancement Report should be sent to the council office immediately following each board of review. This report must be signed by at least three members of the board of review, including its chairman.

   Ships — Explorers in ships should give their advancement applications to their Skipper, who, in turn, takes them before the officers of the ship for approval. Immediately following the approval of the officers, the Skipper should prepare, sign, and forward this Advancement Report to the council office.

2. Only those with unexpired membership certificates can be credited with advancement. Awards are not available to members of units whose charters have expired.
3. Fill in name and only one advancement on each line, but list all of one member's advancement consecutively.
4. When ordering any badges of rank, you must list the names of the boys receiving them.
5. List names of boys who are applying for merit badges and Eagle or Quartermaster awards and attach applications for same to this report.
6. A pack or troop should have a committee member interview boys who are not advancing. List these boys on bottom of form.

FORWARD WHITE AND PINK COPIES TO COUNCIL - KEEP GREEN COPY FOR UNIT FILES

To: Council Advancement Committee
Gentlemen:
I certify that the following record of advancement is correct and meets the standards and requirements of the Boy Scouts of America.

FOR TROOP REPORT: Two additional signatures are required, plus date board of review was held.

BOARD OF REVIEW DATE

_____ Signed _____ Title _____

Name	Qualified for	Name	Qualified for
1.		19.	
2.		20.	
3.		21.	

Chapter Eight

THE LEADERSHIP CORPS

A TROOP may or may not have a leadership corps, as it wishes. Most troops that are eligible to have one do have one.

A leadership corps in your troop would provide these benefits:

- Opportunity for qualified members to learn and apply leadership skills
- Special opportunities for service to Scouting both in and out of the troop and for service outside of Scouting
- Fellowship and activity among older Scouts

Your troop is eligible to form a leadership corps if it has three members who meet the following qualifications:

- Age 14 or 15
- First Class progress award or higher
- Potential leadership, as shown by their activity in the troop since they joined
- Willingness to take special leadership development training and apply it

You can form a leadership corps with as few as three members. The total membership, however, should not be more than a quarter of the total troop membership. If you have 36 Scouts, for example, the leadership corps should not have over nine members.

Leadership corps members do not belong to patrols. Their leader is either the senior patrol leader, an assistant senior patrol leader appointed by him, or an assistant senior patrol leader elected by the leadership corps. The leader of the leadership corps becomes a member of the troop leaders' council.

Once formed, the leadership corps becomes an important resource of the troop and its patrols. The senior patrol leader can call on its members to help with troop meetings and activities. Patrol leaders can call upon the leadership corps for help when needed.

The leadership corps can instruct in Scout skills; help train patrol leaders; lead games, songs, and other activities; and help with troop equipment and records. Members of the leadership corps can hold appointive offices such as scribe, quartermaster, librarian, and den chief.

In addition to its services to the troop, the leadership corps can render service to the council, district, or other troops. It can also render community service outside of Scouting.

Fellowship activities can be any types that appeal to the members. They can be social activities, adventures, trips, sports, or whatever else may appeal.

If you think your troop could qualify to start a leadership corps, talk to your Scoutmaster about it. Get a copy of the booklet *Leadership Corps*, No. 6503, from your local council office. Have a meeting of those who might be eligible and interested and talk it over. Your Scoutmaster will probably be very enthusiastic about the idea.

INDEX